A **WESTERN HORSEMAN** BOOK

Charmayne James
ON BARREL RACING

D1552378

The Complete Training and Conditioning Program of the 11-Time World Champion

---

Written By Charmayne James
With Cheryl Magoteaux

Edited by Kathy Swan
Photography by John Brasseaux
Diagrams by Ron Bonge

Charmayne James

ON BARREL RACING

Published by

WESTERN HORSEMAN® magazine

3850 North Nevada Ave.
Box 7980
Colorado Springs, CO 80933-7980

www.westernhorseman.com

Design, Typography, and Production
Western Horseman
Fort Worth, Texas

Front & Back Cover Photos By
John Brasseaux

Printing
Branch Smith
Fort Worth, Texas

©*2005 by Western Horseman*
a registered trademark of
Morris Communications Corporation
725 Broad Street
Augusta, GA 30901

All rights reserved
Manufactured in the United States of America

Copyright Notice: *This book is copyrighted by Western Horseman and therefore protected by federal copyright law. No material may be copied, faxed, electronically transmitted, or otherwise used without express written permission. Requests must be submitted in writing.*

First Printing: August 2005

ISBN 0-911647-76-7

CONTENTS

FOREWORD

For someone like me, who eats and sleeps barrel racing, what better time to have a career photographing and writing about barrel racing than during the era of Charmayne James. What a privilege it has been to know her, even before she joined the Women's Professional Rodeo Association, and to be able to follow her up through the professional ranks where year after year she sat new records.

The first time I ever heard her name called over a public address system was at the Josey Junior World in Marshall, Texas, in 1983. She was only 13 and just starting out. I was 38 and had seen lots of great barrel horses and riders. Although she barely brushed it, she hit the first barrel leaving it. But her time was fast and her horse impressive. I remember saying to Martha Josey after the first go round was over, "I'm impressed with the bay horse and rider from Clayton, New Mexico. I wonder if they always run that tough."

Being somewhat of a barrel racing historian, I thought it was neat for someone from Clayton to have a good barrel horse. Clayton was where the very first National Finals of the Girl's Rodeo Association, now the Women's Professional Rodeo Association, was held. It made it easy for me to remember Charmayne's home town.

On the Monday following the Josey Junior World I received a call from Charmayne's mom, Gloria James. She wanted to order pictures as they hadn't been many places where there was a photographer. I explained that I had some good ones of her daughter, but that she had lost her hat on every run.

In the two decades that followed, I learned that Charmayne seldom hits a barrel, and I've never seen her lose her hat again.

The records set by Charmayne are well known. I'm proud to have witnessed most of them. I shall forever remember the roar of the crowd inside the Houston Astrodome as she and Scamper rounded the third barrel in the finals to win the championship year after year (10 total). It was a sound, unlike any other place I've been, that sends cold chills up your spine. I've commented time after time as to what a cool hand she was to not "choke," especially at Houston, where 99 percent of the time all she had to do was not hit a barrel in the finals to win the average. As any barrel racer knows, that's a hard assignment.

At the time, I didn't realize what a historical moment it was when Scamper lost his bridle during her run in the seventh go-round at the 1985 National Finals Rodeo. Even though she won the go-round, they were such an outstanding team it was something that you expected of them – win even under the most adverse circumstances. The shot I took of them running home with the bridle between Scamper's legs and Charmayne drawing out her bat captured the moment. I remember thinking "don't goof this shot up, you've only got one chance as she goes by you." That run made the list of most memorable events of the first 20 years of NFRs in Las Vegas.

The amazing thing about Charmayne James is that although she's won 11 world championships, 7 NFR average titles, 10 Houston Rodeo championships and qualified for the Wrangler NFR 19 consecutive years, she's a gracious winner. No one, including her peers, ever tired of her dominance, which speaks volumes about her character as a person, not just her talents as a barrel racer.

Many thought when Scamper started slowing down that Charmayne's interest would change and that she would immediately quit rodeoing. But having seen her compete on a futurity horse that she'd trained herself back in 1987, just as she did Scamper, I knew she'd come back with other winners.

I once asked Charmayne how she could keep traveling thousands of miles, year after year, and not get burned out. Her response was that barrel racing was her job. It was how she made her living. But the other thing she said is probably why she's so respected and has such a good attitude about winning.

"I don't have to win to be happy," were Charmayne's exact words. "I can be satisfied bringing a horse along and knowing that he's doing the best he can do at whatever point he is in his training and development. You can't expect to win first every time. If I'm riding my best and my horse is working his best, then I'm satisfied."

Charmayne James has been important for the sport of barrel racing as a great role model.

Time and time again, when a youth rider who lives in a part of the country far removed from where Charmayne lives or has traveled is interviewed after winning a 4D championship, she quickly gives Charmaynes's name as her favorite or most admired barrel racer. That's impressive.

I've never grown tired of writing about Charmayne, photographing Charmayne or reading about Charmayne. Along with thousands of others, I look forward to reading and rereading the pages that follow.

It's an honor to have known Charmayne James throughout her entire barrel racing career and to watch as she advanced to heights unknown before in all of barrel racing history.

It's an even greater honor to call her my friend.

Kenneth Springer

DEDICATION

To Tony and Tyler Garritano:
You both changed my life for the better. I love you very much!

To my Faith, Family and Friends
and to all the horses that have gone through life misunderstood.

And last, but not least, to the two other loves in my life – Scamper and Cruiser.

ACKNOWLEDGEMENTS

To my husband, Tony Garritano:
Besides being a great husband and father, you do a wonderful job as my manager. I'm very lucky to have you working with me.

To my son, Tyler:
You are a gift from God, and since you've been a part of my life, teaching means so much more. I want to treat kids like I want you to be treated.

To my Mom and Dad, Charlie and Gloria James:
I was very fortunate to grow up in a loving home with parents who loved me and would do anything for me. Dad, you made such a big impression on me with your soft, kind ways with people and horses. Mom, you always told all of us girls that we could do anything, and your tireless help and support was greatly appreciated.

To my Grandmother, Nellie James:
You are such an inspiration to me, not just because you've lived 101 years, but because you are such a kind-hearted person.

To my sisters, Eugenie, Bernadette, Georgina, and my niece, Elizabeth:
I had a great childhood growing up with all of you. Thanks for being a part of my life.

To Larry and Johnette Norris:
First and foremost, you're my very dear friends. Beyond that, you've done a terrific job in helping me build my clinics. Thanks.

To Neil Gibson and Carol Cox:
Thanks for helping me with my business and always looking out for my best interest.

To Randy Reidinger:
You're like a brother I never had. You share my passion for looking out for what's best for the horses.

To Scotty and Becky Wilson:
Scotty, you're truly blessed with the talent you have for fixing horses. Thanks for the work you've done on mine, especially Cruiser, and for the peace of mind you've given me by doing what you do.

To Dr. Richard Godbee:
Your knowledge and insight have benefited me and my students. Thanks.

To Robert Treasure:
Thanks for going beyond the call of duty to keep Cruiser shod the way he needed the year I won the world championship.

To Dr. Robert Lewis:
I love the fact that you treat every person and every horse the same. No matter what person or horse comes into your clinic, they still get the best care. One thing that you taught me is that every person and every horse is important. And above all that, you're just good at what you do.

To Tammy Wallace:
Thank you for your very hard work and your kindness to my students at all my clinics.

To Kenneth Springer:
Thanks for always being there to capture the moment. No one knows barrel racing like you do!

To my late Uncle Frank Brown:
Frank shod Scamper for many years and really helped him a lot.

To all the friends I made on the road:
Those of you who let me stay with you when I was on the road rodeoing, and to all those who helped me through truck breakdowns and let me borrow their rigs, I appreciate you and your kindness.

To all my past sponsors who helped me throughout my career:
Without you it would've been a lot tougher out on the road.

To my present sponsors:
Morinda Corporation, Professional's Choice, Rocky Jeans, Circle M Trailer, and Gore Brothers - I thank you for your continued support.

To Ramiro Benavidez:
I trust you with every horse on the place. You're truly a great horseman, and I appreciate your help.

To Ann Rayburn and Kelley Deibel:
Thanks for being the best babysitters in the world and for your help with Tyler. Neither the book nor the clinics would be possible without the peace of mind that came from knowing he was in good hands.

To John Brasseaux:
Thanks for the great photos in this book. They help bring our words to life.

To Kathy Swan:
Thanks for being a great – and patient – editor!

To Cheryl Magoteaux:
Thanks for getting me up at 5:00 in the morning for a year so we could write this very large book! It wouldn't have been possible at all for me to write this without you. You understood me so well, and I think we developed a close bond that we'll have for the rest of our lives. I just love how you were able to put everything down like I said it. You understood what I meant and then made it make sense. It was so easy to work together, and the steps we went through have helped me become a better teacher as well. Thank you very much.

PREFACE

I was certain that Charmayne James was strong and determined long before I ever met her.

She's earned 19 National Finals Rodeo qualifications in a world where one or two can create life-long celebrity. She won an incredible 11 world championships on two different horses.

There's a lot of available information about her triumphs and her horses, but little about Charmayne. Throughout her career, she's been quiet, composed, willing to let her accomplishments do the talking – and to let her horses take the credit.

I'd read articles about her wins on Scamper and wonder if the writer really thought Scamper dialed PROCOM and entered himself. I'd hear barrel racers talking about how her horse just carried her to the wins – not remembering or caring that she was the one who trained the horse. Sometimes, I suppose, it's just hard for us to accept greatness.

There's no question that Scamper was the best barrel horse, ever. He won 10 world championships, but he didn't do it alone. From the start, Charmayne was his friend, his advocate and his leader. She was willing to go against popular dictates – with a different conditioning program, different feed, different shoeing – because she believed in her horse and knew him better than anyone. Along with the titles, she took the ridicule, the criticism and the unkind remarks and still concentrated on keeping Scamper working and winning light-years longer than any other barrel horse, ever.

But even if you take Scamper out of the picture, Charmayne is still a superstar. Her post-Scamper accomplishments – nine NFR trips and a world championship on Cruiser – move her right back to the head of the class.

So I expected to meet a highly skilled horsewoman. I anticipated brilliance and the ability to focus. I predicted high intelligence and an iron will. I wondered if there was more.

I found that Charmayne does have an incredible ability to stay focused on a goal. She's undeniably brilliant and determined and has the feel and skill that you find in great riders, from any discipline.

But the one quality that made it come together in the beginning – and keeps her captivated now – is the love. She literally falls in love with her horses.

In her mind, Charmayne has a responsibility to help her horses be their best. She believes in them from the start and does whatever it takes to make them succeed. And, now she's turning the same kind of caring and belief to her students.

This book is an attempt to share knowledge and a philosophy of competition, but even more, it's a challenge for you to put your horse first. If you do that, you'll put in the extra hours, make the needed sacrifices and work hard to become as good yourself as you want your horse to be.

Don't be afraid to believe. Don't be afraid of giving it all you have.

If you have the love, the rest will take care of itself.

Cheryl Magoteaux

INTRODUCTION

I wanted to do this book because there's so much information I've learned through two decades of barrel racing.

I'm ready for a new part of my life, and my new challenge is to help barrel racers and their horses. I'm just as devoted now to teaching barrel racing as I was to winning world titles.

Much of what you'll read in this book goes against popular barrel racing theory and technique, but I ask you to give it a chance. Remember, this is a complete program. Each part works because of all the other parts.

Take the time to learn the techniques and methods, and I know they'll help you. Hopefully, this book will become one you read, then re-read. That's important because when you read books for the first time, you sometimes don't completely understand them. Then you go back and read a chapter over and over, and it becomes clearer. Also, the more your skills improve, the more you'll be able to absorb.

You'll be the one who knows what's best for you and your horse. Your horse doesn't need a psychic. He needs you to be as knowledgeable, fair and skilled as possible, and he needs you to take care of his mental and physical needs. This book can show you how.

My goal is to have a student qualify for the National Finals Rodeo. With a lot of work and a little luck, that could be you!

*For a successful career in
barrel racing, you need a solid
foundation in basic horsemanship
and riding skills, and your horse
needs the fundamental training skills
necessary for control at any speed.
This chapter includes quick quizzes
to determine if you and your horse
are ready to run barrels.*

1

BASICS FOR THE HORSE AND RIDER

Good riders constantly improve their riding skills. They work to steady their hands and perfect their reactions, and they enhance their horsemanship knowledge through study and experience.

Horsemanship basics include the ability to cue clearly with your hands and legs and to feel what your horse is doing underneath you. Also, you must have the strength to maintain your seat throughout the acceleration and turns of the pattern and to maintain your balance without pulling on your horse's bridle.

If you can't do this at a walk, trot and lope, you're nowhere near ready to try making a run at world-class speed.

TIPS

Barrel Racing Skills

So what skills should a barrel racer have?

- Be able to clearly communicate to a horse to move forward at a walk, trot, lope and gallop. Ride each gait smoothly and in harmony with the horse.
- Be in control when traveling at any speed. Maintain your seat with your legs while you control your hands and arms for cuing. Your leg strength and stomach muscles should allow you to stabilize your body from the waist down.
- Position your horse's head left to right, controlling the amount of bend to correspond with where you are in the barrel pattern.
- Cue your horse for either lead and know which lead he's on – in front and behind.
- Sit or post a trot and move a horse smoothly from a regular trot to an extended trot.
- Know when a horse responds correctly to your cue, so you stop cuing him.
- Feel your horse as he gathers for a turn and know when and how to ask for more or less rate. "Rate" means the horse adjusts his stride to prepare for a barrel turn.
- Feel any slight deviation from the correct pattern instantly, and correct it before it becomes a major problem.
- Keep your hands steady and smooth and never pull on the reins to balance.

RIDER SKILLS

You have to be honest with yourself in evaluating your riding skills. If you're not comfortable and capable of maintaining control riding at full speed and making a turn, then you can't make a winning barrel run. Even if you buy a super horse and let him pack you around the barrels, you'll likely interfere with him so much that he'll soon stop working because you can't be consistent for him. You'll end up giving him the wrong signals.

There are graduated levels of horsemanship, from beginner to world-class competitor. It's important that your horse match up with your skill levels. It's not unusual to see over-mounted barrel racers riding horses that are way too quick, too aggressive or too intimidating for their level of horsemanship and riding skill. Those riders are out of control when they run barrels.

Be honest about your riding capabilities and strive to partner with a horse that matches your skills. Simply, a beginning rider isn't ready for a top pro rodeo horse. As your riding abilities improve and you develop your timing, you'll be able to get better times out of the horse you're riding. Eventually, you can graduate to a faster horse, if that's your goal. Or, you might find that being a better rider gives you the ability to step your horse up to the next level.

Being able to communicate with your horse is paramount in barrel racing.

TEST
Are You Ready to Run Barrels?

Have someone administer this simple test to you and keep score. Each test is worth five points.

1. From a standstill, clearly cue your horse for a walk by shifting your seat. Deduct a point if you startle the horse, and he doesn't start smoothly. Deduct a point if the horse breaks into a trot or doesn't start at all. If he begins to walk, then breaks into a trot, deduct another point.
2. From a walk, stop your horse with your voice and your body. Five points for a good, relaxed stop where you sit down, say whoa and your horse responds. Deduct a point if you pull on the reins before sitting down in the saddle. Deduct a point if the horse stops and starts again.
3. From a standstill, ask the horse to jog by squeezing with both your calves. Deduct a point if you fail to stop squeezing and cause the horse to speed up. Deduct a point if you can't sit the jog and another point if you can't keep your hands steady.
4. Stop your horse, then walk forward five or six steps before cuing for the right lead with your left heel. Deduct a point if you lean in the direction of the lead, miss a lead, let the horse trot into the lead departure or are unable to keep your hands steady on the reins.
5. Repeat Number 4 for the left lead, cuing with your right heel.
6. Lope your horse in an 80- to 100-foot circle and maintain your seat. Deduct a point for your legs moving back and forth. Deduct a point if your seat is hitting the saddle.
7. Stop your horse from the lope. If you pull on his mouth, or fail to release when he responds, deduct a point for each. If the stop throws you forward, then deduct two points.
8. Go back into the big circle and increase it to the length of the arena so you're loping an oblong circle. Once you're on the long side, ask the horse to increase speed, then smoothly reduce speed on the short ends of the circles. Do this three complete revolutions, going from a lope to a gallop to a lope and back. You'll lose a point for not maintaining your seat or for too much or too little pressure on the bridle or each time you fail to make the speed transitions.
9. On the next straightaway, ask your horse to "whoa." This is worth five points if you don't get thrown forward, which loses you a point. You'll also lose a point for not using your body to cue, and for excessive pulling on the horse or for using the reins before you cue with your voice and body.
10. Starting in the middle of one end of the arena, lope your horse straight down the arena on the left lead. Stop him at the end of the arena. Turn him around and lope back on the right lead. You'll lose a point for the wrong lead or missing the lead either way or not being able to go in a straight line.

Multiply your total by two. Are you an "A" student with a 90 to 100 score or a "D" student with a 60 to 69 who needs to work on acquiring knowledge and body strength?

A good barrel racer should certainly be able to tell which lead her horse is on and know how to stop the horse from any gait. If you don't know when you're on the wrong lead, have a friend watch and tell you until you get the feel.

Here's a hint: During the lope (a three-beat gait), your leg on the leading side feels slightly forward of the other. Listen to the sound of the horse's feet – one, two, three. The shoulder that's up on "three" is the leading shoulder. Ultimately, you'll learn what lead your horse is on by feel alone, without ever having to look down.

TIPS

Improve Your Riding in Your Daily Workout

Sometimes just being aware of your horsemanship helps you improve. When you work your horse each day, concentrate on your seat and hands and the communication with your horse. Here are some tips to improve horsemanship skills.

- Keep light hands – not too high or low. Work on maintaining forward motion by guiding, not pulling straight back.
- Ride with your feet out of the stirrups to work on your balance and seat in the saddle.
- Practice knowing what lead your horse is on at all times.
- Make sure your horse maintains the correct lead in the turn.

- Always sit down before you pick up the reins to cue the horse to stop.
- If your horse braces against you, you're probably hanging on him. Horses learn to pull back when they're pulled on.
- Constantly try to use the least amount of pressure necessary to get the response from your horse. For example, to get the horse to move his body, first try calf pressure, then your heel, then rolling the spur up the side. Do this consistently every time and eventually the horse will respond to the first and mildest cue.

So how do you develop these skills?

There's a simple answer. It all begins with work – spending hours in the saddle, spending time with your horse. This is where you start to pay the price. It's not the glamour part of barrel racing, but really there are only a few glamorous seconds a week, if that much.

If you're having problems with staying stable in your seat, ride without your stirrups to strengthen your legs. Do some exercises to make your stomach muscles stronger. Concentrate on what your hands are doing when you ride. If you ride without a tie-down, your horse will tell you when your hands are rough or non-responsive.

If you love what you're doing, the journey to better horsemanship can be enjoyable. And this is a part of your riding that should never stop. Never quit trying to improve.

HORSE SKILLS

You wouldn't want to get into a car where there were no controls – no accelerator, no steering wheel, no brake pedals.

Why would you want to ride a horse with no basics?

It's surprising how many barrel horses know the pattern, but little else, until you realize how many barrel racers there are who can't even tell what lead their horses are on.

Know what a broke horse feels like. If your horse has some gaps in his education, take the time to re-school him. It'll take a while but will be well worth it.

Rehearse the basics daily with your horse. They're built on four simple building blocks. Teach your horse the basics in the order listed here because each one builds on the one that precedes it.

Give to Pressure

The first basic in the horse's riding foundation is the simple concept of pressure and release from pressure. In the beginning, put pressure on the rein by pulling out to the side. Most likely, the horse will resist by pulling and tossing his head this way and that. When he gives, release the pressure. Soon the horse learns that when he feels pressure, if he softens and gives to it, the pressure disappears. When he does, you've got the first tool in training your horse. But be warned. If you have tough hands, jerk your horse and don't release him when he softens, you'll have exactly the opposite effect. The horse will brace against you and get stiff.

As a rider, you have an awesome responsibility. Realize that a horse learns by repetition – exact repetition. Therefore, you must ask him the same way every time and release when he gives the correct response. If you're distracted, not paying attention and just keep pulling or pull harder when he gives, you'll confuse him.

When you pick up the reins, the horse shouldn't resist. Instead, he should stay soft in the bridle.

The horse should give his head softly to the side, with only light pressure. Remember to stop pulling when he does. The release of pressure is his reward for doing the right thing.

TEST

Is your horse ready to run barrels?

Have someone administer this simple test to you and keep score. Each part is worth five points.

1. Cue your horse to walk and walk him one time around the arena. Five points if he walks forward, relaxed. Deduct a point if he breaks into a trot, doesn't maintain his forward motion, pulls on the bit or tosses his head.

2. Stop your horse. Deduct a point if he starts again on his own, pulls on the bit or tosses his head.

3. Ask for a trot. If he takes more than two steps to trot, deduct a point. More than four steps, deduct another point. Six or more steps, deduct another point. If he breaks into a lope, deduct another. Deduct another if he pulls on the bit or throws his head.

4. Stop your horse. Deduct a point if he starts again on his own, pulls on the bit or tosses his head.

5. Cue your horse to lope on the right lead. If he takes more than two steps to lope, deduct a point. More than four steps deduct another point. Six or more steps, deduct another point. If he charges into a faster trot before loping, or misses the lead, deduct another. Deduct another if he pulls on the bit or throws his head.

6. Cue your horse to lope on the left lead. If he takes more than two steps to lope, deduct a point. More than four steps, deduct another point. Six or more steps, deduct another point. If he charges into a faster trot before loping, or misses the lead, deduct another. Deduct another if he pulls on the bit or throws his head.

7. Walking your horse, ask him to tip his head to the inside and move into a small circle, then with your inside leg and inside rein, increase the size of the circle. Deduct a point is he fights the bit or moves his head. Deduct one if he fails to move out from the leg and rein pressure.

8. Ask the horse to back. Backing straight until you release the reins is worth five points. Take away a point if he throws his head, a point if he opens his mouth, a point if he stops and a point if he backs crooked.

9. Cue the horse to lope, then reduce and increase the speed of the circle. Deduct a point if he won't slow down and a point if he won't speed up.

10. Cue the horse to lope, then reduce and increase the size of the circle. Deduct a point if he won't move in and a point if he won't move out. Also, remember to keep his body shaped in line with the size of circle.

Multiply your final score by two. Is your horse an "A" student – in the 90 to 100 score range – that's ready to work barrels? Or is he a 70-percent "C" student that could use some review before going further? If you're already running your horse and he can't pass this test, you now have plenty to do in your schooling time each day!

You're actually doing two things in teaching this simple skill. One, you're training the horse to give to pressure and bend to the side. But just as important, you're teaching him that your cues are a request. If he gives the right answer, he gets the reward of released pressure. It's a small thing, but the basis for everything you'll ever teach your horse. He'll be confident throughout his career if he understands your cues and knows the correct answers.

That confidence comes from repetition. After you give the same cue a thousand times, your horse is really going to trust you. However, if, at that point, you have a temper overload and jerk on him for no reason, he'll know you were lying all along.

Ride for the horse – for what you want him to be. Have faith in him, be consistent and your efforts will pay off. Outside influences, moods, or anger don't have any place in the training pen.

At first, ask for just a little "give" to the side. As the horse learns more and becomes more confident, you can ask for a greater bend. Eventually, you can ask him to keep his head in whatever position you put it. Also, as he develops the ability to feel you softly put pressure on a rein, you'll be able to gradually move your hand in closer to the horse – picking up instead of pulling straight out to the side – and still get the same response.

Always remember to work on one side at a time, then do something else. Later, come back and school the other side. Because of the way horses learn (they have two sides to their brains), trying to teach the bend both ways at the same time makes the process take longer.

Giving to the bit side-to-side instead of resisting pressure is the first skill of a broke horse.

Giving at the Poll

The second skill is for the horse to give at the poll. In other words, when you pick up the reins, the horse stays soft in the bridle, tucking his head slightly.

You teach this skill the same way, building on the principle you instilled in the first basic. Apply straight-back rein pressure, as you squeeze with both your calves and just hold steady. The horse's first response is usually, "Hey, you're asking me to whoa and go at the same time." This is where the learned response of finding a release from pressure comes in.

Because the horse is already comfortable with giving his head side-to-side, he'll move his head to different positions to find the right "answer" to your request. Eventually, he'll drop his nose, and, when he does, immediately reward him by releasing the pressure. Once he learns the concept, you'll eventually be able to put his head where you want it.

You're not asking for the ultra-tucked headset of a show horse. As a matter of fact, it's not about a headset at all. You simply want your barrel horse to have a tool to keep soft in the bridle.

You can tell if the horse has been previously ridden by a bad-handed rider because the first thing he'll do when he feels you pick up the reins is throw his head into a nose-out position. He expects the bridle to hurt him, and by nosing out, he feels less vulnerable. In that position, bad hands don't hurt him as much as when his nose is down.

As you develop this skill, you'll also notice that the horse's conformation changes. Having a horse break at the poll lengthens and strengthens the top line from poll to withers, while softening the muscles under the neck. Ultimately, when you look at a horse, you can tell how much he resists the bridle just by looking at his conformation.

This skill is very important for barrel horses because of how you shape for a turn, with the horse's front end elevated and his nose slightly tipped inside. If the horse's head is up and out and the back is arched, you can't maintain this shape.

Of course, there are extremes, too. If a horse's head is tucked to his chest, he can't work either. He must break at the poll to maintain proper shape without arching his back. It helps the horse's longevity when you don't make him sore from being in bad body position.

Move Away from Leg Pressure

The third basic skill for the horse to learn is to move away from leg pressure. Ride the horse forward squeezing slightly with both your legs, then release one leg – moving it deliberately away from the horse as you continue pressure with the other leg. Think of it as opening a door for your horse to move through as you push with the other leg. If you feel him move even slightly away from the pressure, release. Then repeat a couple of hundred times or more until he understands and moves smoothly away from leg pressure.

Move Out Laterally

As your horse develops the skill of moving away from your leg, also teach him the fourth needed skill – to move out laterally from an inside rein. You don't want to actually move your horse out in the barrel pattern, but instilling awareness of the inside rein helps your horse maintain his position going into the turns.

Begin at a walk, with your horse's head slightly tipped to the inside and body shaped inside. Maintain pressure on the outside rein to prevent your horse from turning to the inside or tipping his head too much at the same time you pick up the inside rein and angle it across his neck. Use your inside leg to help your horse understand the cue. Soon, however, he'll be able to move to the outside just from the guiding inside rein. Ultimately, your hand on the inside rein at the barrel helps guide him, and he won't drop into the turn when you have that barrier up.

Skills Needed For Specific Barrel Problems

Those four skills – and the ability to walk, trot, lope and stop on cue – are all the skills you need to run barrels. Any time you find a problem in the barrel pattern, you can trace it to one of those basics breaking down.

For example, if your horse runs past the barrels, work him on giving at the poll. That reinforces the rate, ("Rate" means the horse adjusts his stride to prepare for a turn around the barrel.) helps him be receptive to your cues and reinforces softness in the bridle.

If he's not staying shaped around a barrel, review him on giving his head side-to-side. Do this work away from the barrels so he responds to the cue instead of the pattern.

If your horse ducks in around a barrel too early, you're likely releasing the outside rein too soon, or he's not comfortable with guidance from the rein. Review the basic of giving at the poll, while maintaining a straight line. Think about the problem and then isolate what might be the basic tool that would correct it.

Throughout the pattern, your horse should accept your guidance. In the approach to each barrel, he should be soft and make a smooth transition from running speed to turning speed in response to you picking up on the reins.

Also, don't go through the barrel pattern and pull your horse into the ground to a stop in front of the barrel. That just scares him and teaches him to dread and regard that part of the pattern as a place where something bad can happen. You don't want him to stop at the barrel anyway.

The pattern is the most integral part of barrel racing. Although some arenas are longer or wider or have softer or harder ground, the pattern is always the same and your approach to it should never change. Your ability to be a great barrel racer is based completely on how you're able to see and run the exact same pattern over and over again, exactly the same way. This helps the horse learn in the beginning; and once the horse is seasoned, it keeps him working correctly.

2

PATTERN
AND
POSITION

Horses learn by repetition – exact repetition. If you approach the pattern the same way every time, have the same posture every time, use your body and hands to cue the same way every time, then your horse learns to run exactly the same pattern every time. He's never confused or unsure about what his job is. But if you're inconsistent in what you're doing, then your horse is going to be uncertain. As you ask him to go faster, he'll be overcome by the run and not understand that he should take responsibility for rating. He'll drop in to the barrel or resist with his face. Other problems will arise.

Remember, horses are reassured by repetition, but they're stressed by inconsistency. And the last place you want to stress your horse is around the barrels.

The Basic Pattern

For something that's so simple, it's a wonder that it can seem so complex. Barrel racers go straight, turn right, go straight, turn left, go straight, turn left, go straight, then stop. It's amazing that we, as riders, can transform something this elementary into something so daunting.

I have one basic pattern for running barrels, but there are also variations, based on different arenas. In this chapter, I'll start out with the most basic pattern, then address variations, corrections and adjustments.

My perfect pattern has five imaginary axis points around half the perimeter of each barrel. These are points I ride around as I turn each barrel. Get out a pencil and make this drawing for yourself. (See "The Perfect Pattern" diagram.) Connect the axis points, and you'll see a perfect pattern. Eliminate any one of the points and see what your pattern looks like. Take out two of them and you compound the problem.

The distance away from the barrels at each axis point is three to four feet – the same distance all the way around the barrel. This varies slightly depending on your horse, his size and turning style. If you ride too close or too wide at any one of the axis points – instead of staying the uniform distance from the barrel – it distorts the turn and affects how fast you complete the barrel and set up for the next one.

Just before each of the first axis points, there's a transition area (the darkened area shown on the diagram) where you collect and rate down to prepare for the turn. In the transition area and around each barrel, you should sit down in your saddle. Make sure your tailbone is pushing down into the saddle and that you're not putting too much weight into your stirrups. More about the transition area later.

Where To Look

In turning a barrel, the first rule is never, ever look at the barrel! Instead, look where you're about to run. You'll have to, anyway, to see and cover all the axis points.

Think of driving a car. If you're driving down the highway and look over at the side of the road, you usually subconsciously steer toward it. Looking directly at the barrel seems to have the same effect. Often, when I find a rider having problems hitting barrels, getting her to change where she looks is all it takes to fix the problem. Horses are so incredibly tuned in to riders. They feel our bodies and can tell where we're looking by our body language and also because our hands follow our eyes. After a horse has been ridden for a while, you can almost steer it completely just by where you look.

Try it sometime. Warm up your horse and get him really relaxed and tuned in to you. Then, just walk around, with the reins loose. Don't move your body; just look where you want to go. Most horses react to that right away by following in the direction you look.

Just like you don't want to look at the side of the road, you don't want to look down at the dashboard or steering wheel either. If you look down, you lose track of where you're going. How many times have you seen someone

The Perfect Pattern.

The dots indicate the axis points and the X's indicate the most important points to look at. The solid line in front of Axis Point #1 at each barrel is the transition area.

What Happens if You Miss the Axis Points

Study the diagram titled "The Perfect Pattern." On each turn around the barrel, there are points that you must ride over. If you miss one, you'll flatten the turn, lose forward motion and possibly knock down a barrel. Always look ahead to your next point.

The solid line indicates the position that can cause horses to come out wide or even duck off. The broken line indicates the correct barrel pattern and most riders' intended route, but many barrel racers lose this position by looking at the barrel or down the inside of the horse's neck. This distorts your perspective because you can't properly guide the horse while looking down to the inside. You need to look ahead over the top of his head, as you guide him to every axis point around the barrel.

To prevent this loss of position, guide while keeping your horse's head under your line of sight and your hands in front of you – not too low or high, never pulling straight back and never pulling the horse's head to the side. Also, never pull the horse away from the barrel as pulling him away from the barrel makes him drop his shoulder into the barrel.

Riders are often taught to push the horse coming into the turn to keep from hitting the barrel. But if the rider does that, the horse often gets frustrated, passing the barrel and running up the fence. The broken line is the correct position.

A horse that shoulders or comes in too close to the second or third axis points misses most of the rest of the axis points. Again, the solid line is the incorrect course; the broken line is the correct position.

looking down, maybe to pick up an over-and-under or bat, then they look up and have to make a big steering correction?

Looking at the Right Axis Points the Wrong Way

You can't guide your horse if you look at the wrong spot – or even if you look at the right spot incorrectly. It's essential that you look ahead over the horse's head. If you need

to, use his ears as a focal point below your line of sight.

If instead, you look down the inside of your horse's neck at the axis points, rather than ahead, you're looking at a different perspective than your horse and lose sync with him.

Many riders have been taught to turn and look at the next barrel from behind the barrel to finish the turn tighter and faster. This doesn't work because your hands follow your eyes, so

TIPS

Pattern Rules

- Never, ever look at the barrel. Instead, look where your horse is going to step next, just as if you were running on foot.
- If you've been looking at the barrels and have trouble looking at the ground, try using your horse's ears as a focal point to look through at your next step around the barrel. Be sure to keep the horse's head under your line of sight. Keep in mind that if you've been looking at the barrels, it'll be a hard habit to break. However, with enough practice, you'll automatically react correctly.
- Keep your horse the same distance all the way around the barrel – think of a perfect circle that's approximately three feet away all the way around.
- Keep your hands forward in the turn. Horses hate a hard pull. The key is to guide around the turn, not to stop the forward motion and pull the horse around. Experiment with how much rein pressure you need to have your horse make the turn. With some horses, your hands are there as a guide. Others might need more than that.

- Timing is one of the hard-to-define qualities of a good barrel racer and comes from spending many years developing good hands and a feel of knowing when to make contact and how much.
- Around the barrel is where you should be the smoothest with your hands and the steadiest in your seat.
- With an inexperienced horse, always ride two-handed until the horse is trained and knows the pattern well.
- Teach a horse rate by shortening his stride. You can do that at a trot or gallop by always going slower around the barrels than you do between them. If the horse slows down or goes the same speed in a turn, he keeps his hindquarters controlled and collected. If he speeds up in the turn, his rear end pushes rather than sets, and that causes a horse to become inconsistent and unable to maintain a smooth turn.

Looking Wrong

Arrow lines are where the rider incorrectly looks to the inside. The dotted line indicates where the rider should look – over the top of the horse's head rather than down his neck.

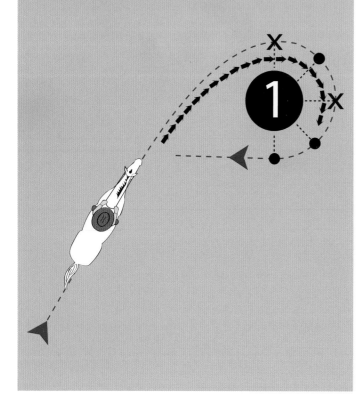

you pull your horse before his hindquarters have had a chance to come around the barrels. When you don't let the horse's back end complete the turn properly, you slow down your run. You miss the last axis points around the barrel that are so crucial to completing the turn fast. Remember, the hindquarters are where the horse gets his power. Your horse must be collected, or you can either come out wide or hit the barrel. Even if you don't hit the barrel, you lose momentum and time because your horse has to take an extra step. This can also cause the horse to crossfire and be out of position so he doesn't have the power and momentum to leave the turn strong.

Large Pockets

In the turn, the ideal is to stay the same distance away from the barrel all the way through. One popular theory is to make a big pocket going into the barrel and coming out close, but I've found that coming out close causes the horse to miss Axis Points #4 and #5 and ultimately forces the horse to lose his shape in the last part of the turn.

Riding large pockets around barrels can cause you to do three things. First, it makes the horse drop his shoulders more. Second, it slows your time because your horse has to make more steps around the barrel. Third, you can hit the barrel.

Looking Up Too Soon

Look at these two photos. The horses are in the same position, but the difference is where the rider is looking. In the photo on the left, I look where I want my horse to go, to finish guiding her around the turn. In the second photo, the rider looks up at the next barrel too soon. This causes her to be out of time and unaware of where her horse's head is. Keeping your horse's head under your line of sight will help you to guide your horse.

1. The horse is in good position to complete the turn, and if the rider continues to guide the horse, it will be correct.

2. But if the rider looks up and either begins to kick or assumes a "go" body position that tells the horse to go fast before the turn is complete, he'll loose postition and miss Axis Points #3 and #4.

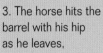

In the next step, because of this lost position the horse does one of three things:

3. The horse hits the barrel with his hip as he leaves,

4. or the horse comes out wide to get past the barrel.

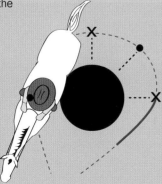

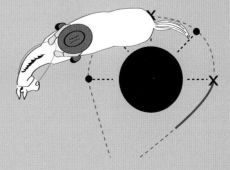

The horse might stay somewhat on course, but move his back end away to clear the barrel, therefore slowing his time. He's likely to cross-fire if he steps his hip out. He's lost the forward motion.

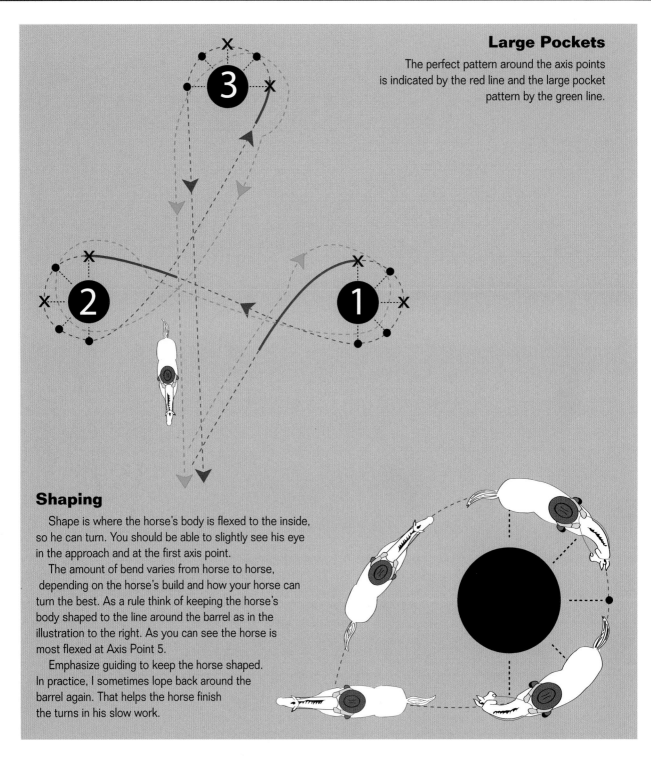

Large Pockets

The perfect pattern around the axis points is indicated by the red line and the large pocket pattern by the green line.

Shaping

Shape is where the horse's body is flexed to the inside, so he can turn. You should be able to slightly see his eye in the approach and at the first axis point.

The amount of bend varies from horse to horse, depending on the horse's build and how your horse can turn the best. As a rule think of keeping the horse's body shaped to the line around the barrel as in the illustration to the right. As you can see the horse is most flexed at Axis Point 5.

Emphasize guiding to keep the horse shaped. In practice, I sometimes lope back around the barrel again. That helps the horse finish the turns in his slow work.

Often, when making a pocket, the rider actually moves the horse away from the barrel in the approach (shown in barrel #2 in the "Large Pockets" diagram), causing him to drop his shoulders back in to make the turn. Soon, the horse begins to anticipate and drop even more.

Even if the approach to the pocket is straight and correct, finishing the back side of the barrel so closely causes the horse to lose his shape and momentum and doesn't allow him to leave the turn as powerfully.

Shape

The horse's body should be shaped to the part of the barrel he's on. At Axis Point #1, he's just beginning to bend, but at Axis Points #4 and #5, he's in his most curved position, then maintains some shape until the turn is completed. Think of a train track around the barrel.

If your horse is bent too much to the inside, or not bent enough, he'll run off the track.

To get the horse to bend, use inside rein pressure and a little inside leg pressure. As you turn the barrel with your inside leg gripping slightly, you'll have more weight in your outside stirrup. But, don't overdo your legs or your hands. When you get the desired response, that's enough. Remember, once the horse has learned, he does a lot of this on his own, and you have to cue less.

It's easy to over-bend and when that happens, it's like a car putting on the breaks with the wheels turned way to the inside, causing the car to skid out away from the turn. You lose time.

If the horse doesn't maintain the shape of the curve, it causes problems. For example, if he straightens up too soon, he can't get his hip past the barrel he's leaving.

When I talk about getting to the axis points, I mean to get the horse's body there, not just his head. You must point your horse's head in the correct position. His shoulders and hips will follow in a fluid motion.

It's the horse's body you should guide, not his head. A horse can't run a correct pattern if you just get his head to the axis points. You must get his body to follow these points, so be sure to ride and guide for the horse, not the head.

This is so important. A horse has four legs, not two and his rear legs are a long way from the head. You're over the legs, and to develop timing you have to learn to ride where you are, not where the horse's nose is.

Of course, you use the horse's head to guide and position the horse, and the horse uses his head and neck to balance. However, you should have the perspective of where his body is and how his feet are hitting the ground. Guide your horse to the position where you want the inside hind foot to land. If you can, push down with your inside tailbone and get your seat in time with the horse hitting the ground with his inside hind foot. This might be confusing if you're not an experienced rider, but as your skills increase this is something to work toward.

When riding a barrel horse, you're the driver. That's your job. The horse is the engine, and his very complicated task is to react immediately to your cues and guidance while running as fast as he can. A horse becomes more confident if you guide him smoothly, looking over his ears ahead to where you're going. If he

begins to drop in too early and you're looking on the line straight ahead where you want to go, you feel the mistake immediately and can correct it while it's still a simple, small adjustment. By the same token, if you look down his neck, or look at the barrel, you don't realize right away that your horse has gotten out of position. Then, it's either too late to correct or the correction is so big it slows the run.

Many riders have been told to look at the pocket or the beginning of the barrel turn. So, they look at the pocket until they can't see it; then they look right at the barrel, which causes them to lose smoothness and momentum. There are very few horses that can keep working correctly under those circumstances.

TIPS

The Five Biggest Things to Remember

Here are the five things that will help your barrel racing the most.
- Never look at the barrel.
- Never look down the horse's neck.
- Keep on the perfect route; stay the same distance from the barrel and hit every axis point all the way around each barrel.
- Keep your hands soft and guiding instead of rough and disruptive.
- Don't look at the next barrel until you've completely finished with the turn you're at.

Hand Position

Depending on the horse, you shape more or less going into the barrel. Here, riding one-handed around the first barrel, I have a little more inside rein.

I'm riding Indigo one-handed around the first barrel. Note the light contact on the reins, just guiding him around.

I'm riding Cruiser two-handed around the first barrel. Note how my hands are elevated but I'm sitting down, close to my horse. His body is in the proper position, and I'm looking ahead at where I want him to go.

Leaving the first barrel, both hands are forward. I'm squeezing with my legs and letting him run. Do this leaving all three barrels to get the most run. Also, if you release the pressure on the horse completely to leave, it's easier for him to feel when you pick up for the next turn.

When to Use One or Two Hands Around the Barrel

Between the barrels, I ride mostly two-handed, but your horse's stage of training and his style of running will determine whether you ride with one hand or two hands around the barrel.

If I am on an inexperienced horse, I like to ride two-handed in the turns to guide him and keep him in the correct position in the turn until he learns his position.

Even once he learns it, I ride him two-handed when I compete on him. This is very important because most horses tend to look around, and you can't guide them and help them as well with one hand alone. And they'll need more help guiding when they go to a new environment.

This way of riding is reassuring to the horse; I'm helping him build his confidence by consistently being there to guide him.

One thing to remember any time you ride two-handed: When you shape the horse's head on the back of the barrel, give with your outside rein at the last axis points. If you don't, you're asking the horse to bend with your inside rein and preventing him from doing so with your outside.

Later, I start riding one-handed around the barrels because the horse has been taught correct position and is able to maintain it on his own.

Go two-handed to the barrel, and, as you approach the turn, sit down and drop the outside rein and hold on to the saddle horn with your outside hand to stay steady.

Continue to guide with the inside rein and, depending on how much shape you need with your horse, you can lift your hand and twist your wrist up (as if you were looking at your fingernails) or bring your hand slightly to the side.

Note: The horse whose reins you lift and twist is the one that needs a little more shape in the turn.

With a horse that has more bend, bring your hand out to the side a little. That gives more indirect rein pressure, which helps prevent too much bend. (Note: the exception to this would be with a non-shank bit and a very long rein. In this situation, pulling out to the side would still get the bend.)

The transformation that takes place going to the barrel two-handed and changing to one hand for the turn is such a great cue and is effortless for the rider. Turning the barrel one-handed is a great way to not interfere but still guide your horse.

When you ride one-handed around the barrels, this is the starting position for tipping the horse's nose to the inside.

Here a twist of the wrist makes contact to slightly tip the horse's head to the inside without much pressure on the outside rein.

Sometimes, I ride a finished horse two-handed. That would be one like Cruiser, who was "bendy" and needed guiding. I'd also ride two-handed on a horse that wouldn't maintain position distance all the way around a barrel.

Also, if you've been looking at the barrel and not giving your horse sufficient room, you'll need to ride two-handed to get through the process and get your horse tracking in the proper position again.

Experiment with your horse to see if he runs better with one hand or two in the turn. I believe that, in most cases, you should guide to the barrel with both hands, then go to one

Mechanics of the First Barrel Turn Riding Two-Handed

1. With an inexperienced horse or one that's having some problems, it's important to ride two-handed. Remember to keep your hands up, not down, and to guide, not pull.

2. The horse is in the correct position with his body shaped to the turn. If you drew a line of where he's going, you'd see that his body position fits the shape of the line exactly.

3. My hands are elevated to lift and shape up and around.

4. I remain seated and squeeze with my legs to help the horse complete the turn. Don't think you just need to get the horse's head around the turn, and look up and leave. You've got to get your body (and the horse's body) clear before the turn is finished.

Mechanics of the First Barrel Turn Riding One-Handed

1. In this approach, my horse (Charlie) is rating, and I have gone to riding with one hand. I guide with one hand, lifting the rein and twisting my wrist to the inside.

2. This shows that I'm looking at, and getting to, the axis points.

3. Because my horse was in proper position, he's now collected and can leave the barrel with power, therefore, stopping the clock.

Mechanics of the Second Barrel Turn Riding Two-Handed

1. My horse (Captain) is slightly shaped in the approach. I look over the top of his head to where we're going. Remember, never look to the inside down your horse's shoulder. You wouldn't drive a car looking out the side window instead of the windshield.

2. Since I'm riding with both hands, I can control the amount of bend. Because I'm looking over the top of his head, I can feel any slight deviation from the correct route, and correct it before it develops into a mistake that would make me miss an axis point.

3. As we get into the turn, I keep him collected and shaped a little more.

4. I guide him to each axis point.

5. I still look over the top of his head and still sit steady in the turn.

6. We complete the turn.

Mechanics of the Second Barrel Turn Riding One-Handed

2. I still guide softly.

1. My horse (Sea Doo) approaches the barrel in good position. Notice in this entire sequence that I look over the top of his head so he and I are in sync throughout the turn.

4. I really sit deep in the turn, allowing my horse to keep his hindquarters underneath himself.

3. My hands are light and don't inhibit my horse's progress.

5. I pick up on him a little to finish the back side of the turn.

Mechanics of the Third Barrel Turn Riding Two-Handed

1. On the approach, I collect my horse (Grasshopper) and sit down. His nose is now slightly tipped to the inside.

2. This shows how I've tipped his nose slightly more, using a little more pressure with the calf of my inside leg, as well, to help him maintain the correct position around the back side of the turn.

Mechanics of the Third Barrel Turn Riding One-Handed

1. On The Crown Dancer, I lift the reins and look to my axis points around the barrel.

2. As we've gotten into the turn, she needs less help so I just guide.

3. I'm still just guiding.

4. I complete the turn with soft, guiding hands.

Riding Two-Handed on a Green Horse

1. I've got Captain collected with his nose tipped slightly. I use a little pressure with the calf of my inside leg to help him maintain his shape. My hands are forward, asking him to move ahead.

2. I start more of the turn and have slightly increased the amount of inside rein pressure.

3. We continue the turn. Captain stays soft and guides well.

Pulling Out to the Side

4. As I complete the sharpest part of the turn, I softly ask him for more bend, using inside leg pressure.

With the hand pulling to the inside, it puts pressure on the outside rein. The inside rein still helps guide, while the pressure from the off-rein helps steady a too-bendy horse.

Riding Two-Handed on a Finished Horse

1. As I start the turn I'm riding with two hands sitting, looking over the top of Cruiser's head. My hands are up and forward, not pulling down toward my leg, even at this point, when I'm shaping him to the inside.

2. Through the turn, using both hands lets me keep him shaped. I keep my hands up, instead of pulling down.

3. I still have him shaped and am beginning to complete the turn. This is the part of the turn where the horse is the most flexed.

hand in the turn. This allows you to guide your horse as he's going in a straight line.

In the turn, holding the horn helps you stabilize your body and steady the rein hand so you can clearly and smoothly cue, instead of having your hand involuntarily moving from the motion of the turn. With less experienced horses, though, I ride two-handed all the way through the pattern to give the horse confidence and to help him maintain his position. You can experiment going with one hand but if you lose your position, go back to two.

As a general rule, until a horse is really solid, I like to ride him two-handed all the way through the pattern. That gives him a little more security and makes for a longer career.

The Transition Area

One of the most important aspects of running a perfect pattern is the transition area. That is the speed-change area where the horse collects for the turn, shortens his stride and gathers up. It begins at what I call the braking point and ends at Axis Point #1, the beginning of the turn.

The location of the beginning of the transition depends on how much room it takes you to make the speed change and have the horse gathered and ready to make the turn by Axis Point #1.

The length of that transition area depends on the type of horse, the ground and the length of the run to the barrel. Harder running horses or long-strided horses usually need a little more space to collect. Horses that are not so free-running generally need less transition space.

The ground has an effect on how much room it takes to change speeds and collect. When the ground is hard, horses need to shut down early. Not only are they running faster on hard ground but also when it comes time to put on the brakes, shallow ground doesn't hold them as well. Likewise, if you have a horse with a lot of rate, in deep ground, you might have to ride more aggressively to keep him from losing his momentum in the deep ground going into the turn.

Overall, it's easier for a horse to gather up in a short distance, but, if the horse has a longer distance to run and is really stretched out, it takes more distance to shut down and shorten his stride.

Timing of the transition is very important. Think of driving a car around a curve. If you apply the brakes too early, you slow down too

Transition Area

The Transition Area is from the beginning of the rate to the place where you turn. Remember to guide with both reins in the transition area, then go to one hand in the turn. These transition strips will vary slightly in length because all horses rate at different spots.

The transition strips shown below best suit the horse that really likes to collect and rate for the turns.

These transition strips are longer. Notice how close the beginning of the transition strip is to the timer line. This best suits young horses, free runners, or horses having trouble rating or collecting.

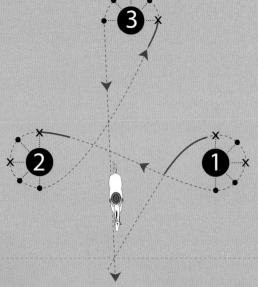
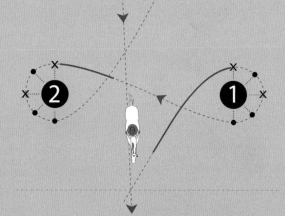

1. This shows the approach to the transition area. I still haven't asked my horse Jazz to rate for the turn.

2. When I sit down at the beginning of the transition area Jazz responds by rating and preparing for the turn. The point that the transition area begins depends on the horse, how much rate he has, and how much room it takes for him to collect himself.

3. Once I sit down in the transition area, I stay down all the way around.

4. As you can see, when I'm riding a young horse, like Grasshopper, he requires more transition area to give him room to shorten his stride for the turn.

much. If you don't apply them soon enough, you skid past the turn.

You ask for the transition or rate by your body position. Sit down on your horse, don't lean back, but let your back soften and slump. Keep your body and shoulders straight, not leaning in or out. When your horse feels your body shift, it becomes his cue to get in position to turn, as well.

Depending on the horse, you might also add rein pressure or a voice cue. Your goal is to bring about adequate speed reduction to get around the turn. Then, as you round the curve and finish the turn, you accelerate again.

Remember the car analogy. You don't stomp on the brakes one time going into the turn, then skid around it. Same way with the horse – you don't jerk on the reins one time going in then just drop them. Your goal is to make the shortest and smoothest transition that your particular horse and the particular arena will allow because that lets you be the fastest.

If you slow down too early, two things can happen. One, you won't correct the error and you'll likely come in toward the barrel too much and miss your first axis point. The other is that you try to correct by speeding back up. Then it's easy to go past the barrel. That's another reason why timing is so important!

Remember, too, that the transition area for the first barrel is going to be longer than the second or third. That's because of the adrenalin the horse has going to the first and because running to the second and third is usually more like running to a barrel that sits in front of a fence. Also, approaching the fence causes most horses to collect more.

Different Approaches for Different Arenas

Check out any arena with a side gate long before the race and pick your place to start. When it's time to run, ride right to that spot that will give you a nice arc to the first barrel. Move purposefully to the point you've picked out – keeping forward motion – then, when you reach that spot, begin your run.

Some arenas are narrow, so there' s not much distance between the first and second barrels. If that's the case, you'll stay straight a little longer before beginning the arc. That will prevent you from getting too far over before it's time to make your turn.

Conversely, if the pattern is wide between the first and second barrels, you will begin sooner to make more of a gradual arc.

In either case, adjust the arc so that you end up in the transition area in the right shape to make the turn.

Correct Rider Body Position

Your posture in the saddle while running the barrels is important. Watch a jockey ride. He's in time with his horse's stride because the last thing he wants to do is cause the horse to slow down.

First of all, ride with your hands forward, soft on the reins and with arms slightly bent at the elbows. This is a non-interference posture in time with the horse's stride, just like a jockey's.

Throughout a barrel run, your midsection is a shock absorber separating you from top to bottom. It absorbs the movement and impact of the running horse while allowing your hands

Narrow and Wide Patterns

If the pattern is narrow between the first and second barrel, stay straight a little longer.

If the pattern is wide between the first and second barrels, begin the gradual arc sooner.

Walk-In Pattern

X – Starting point
0 – Starting point for a large pattern
Begin your run lined up with third barrel shown at point X. For a larger pattern, start your run just to the inside of the straight line from the starting point to the third barrel.

Offset Pattern

This is the best point to take off for the first barrel for an offset-pattern that's not square with the arena and has a side entrance. You can see the first barrel and you're centered with the third.

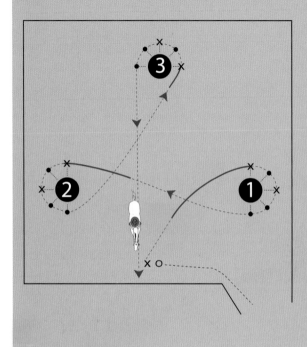
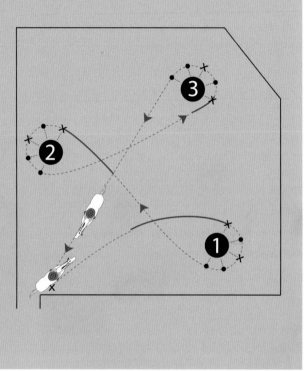

and legs to be soft and stable. Your legs shouldn't be stiff. Use them to slightly grip your horse or bump to urge him forward.

In the transition area and in the turn, sit on your pockets with your back slightly bent. Stay soft to take up the concussion as you keep contact with the saddle. In fact, melt down in the saddle, but keep your shoulders and body square. Don't lean back. Don't ride braced and cocked away from the horse, and don't ride with one of your ears closer to your shoulders than the other one. All these are positions for which the horse has to compensate.

Finally, if you've been looking at the barrel or have been too aggressive with your hands, understand that fixing the problem will take a while. You have to re-train your muscle memory and that takes time. You'll get to the point where you can be correct at home but at an event where you get a little nervous, you revert to the old habit. Keep working at it. Eventually you will retrain yourself, and new habits will replace old ones.

The First Barrel

Now that I've discussed all the basics to running a pattern, let's put it all together and make a run.

Picture your approach to the first barrel from the alleyway. Walk into the alley and get the feel so you don't have surprises coming in. Decide where you want to stop.

Watch some other horses go. If you don't see any of them running by or hitting barrels, you know that the arena doesn't have a tendency to make horses do that. On the other hand, if you see a lot of mistakes, try to figure what might be causing them.

For example, say your center alleyway sets off to the left. In this case, many horses have a tendency to fade more if they have to run over to the right. Be sure you maintain your position looking at your axis points no matter what angle you're coming from.

Your first barrel sets up your run. In most cases, you begin your pattern from a starting place centered with the third barrel. Line up your approach with the third barrel and gradually arc to the first barrel. The arc helps make the pattern flow and allows the horse to maintain a little more speed in the turn without unnecessary impact and torque. Also, the gradual arc helps keep the horse's body shaped and in correct position for a smoother, faster turn that stops the clock.

Consider how fast you should take off to the first barrel. If your horse is very excitable and has a lot of run and not a lot of rate, move up as close to the timer as possible, keeping the horse as relaxed as possible before the run. Try not to lean forward or inadvertently cue your horse to take off. Keep him calm. Slow down your actions.

Your arc to the first barrel depends on how far the barrel is from the starting line. If it's a short way to the first barrel, start your arc right away. If it's farther out, stay straighter longer. If the arena is narrow, you'll stay in the center a hair longer.

Through your first turn, your hands should be forward. Have three to four feet to the left of the first barrel and maintain that same distance all the way around the barrel. Sit straight in the saddle; don't lean. Your head should be square with your shoulders as you

focus through the horse's ears with your hands forward, guiding, not pulling back. Don't look at the barrel. Instead, look ahead to your axis points where you want the horse to go.

How and where you start your horse running to the first barrel depends on a lot of factors. At the fairgrounds in Oklahoma City, for example, where you come down a long alley and it's a pretty long way to the first barrel, you wait as long as possible and make sure your horse is "locked in" to the first barrel before you let him go. Of course, with a finished horse, this isn't as necessary; a good barrel horse comes in hunting the first barrel. However, at the National Finals Rodeo, which takes place in the Thomas & Mack Arena in Las Vegas, you don't have that luxury. It's a blind alley and you have to be running before you can even see the first barrel.

The Second Barrel

Coming off the first barrel, site down the line to a point three to four feet to the side of the second barrel and run a straight line to that point. When you leave the first barrel, get both hands on the reins and keep your horse's head under your line of sight.

Sitting down for the turn.

The "GO" position.

As you go across the arena, if your horse feels like he's fading in too much toward the second barrel, guide him with both reins to keep him standing up. Remember, you can't keep the position you want with the inside rein alone. You must guide with two hands, looking over your horse's head to the correct axis point.

When you approach the second barrel at axis point one, you'll sit down and if you're going to go around the barrel one-handed, this is where you'll drop to one hand. Dropping the outside rein too early can result in loss of position.

Keep looking ahead to each next axis point over the horse's head all the way around the turn. Remember, if you look down the horse's shoulder or over at the barrel, your hand drops, the horse's body comes over and the horse doesn't finish with a nice smooth turn. Miss a point on the axis and you'll lose time or hit a barrel.

The second barrel is one that's often hit, and sometimes a rider who hits barrels tries to overcome that by looking past the barrel at the fence. However, if she looks at the fence, her horse still doesn't know what she wants him to do. The rider can become afraid to touch her horse because when she does, he drops in, so she tries to go fast and get past the point of hitting the barrel.

That method might work at first but then it makes the problem worse because after a few such runs the horse starts to figure it out. He thinks, "Okay, we're going to run in straight, then drop in really hard."

I feel strongly that if you have a problem, you don't correct it by going faster. If you can't be correct going slow, you sure can't fix your problem going fast.

The Third Barrel

If you leave the second barrel correctly, you're set up for a perfect third barrel.

When you leave the second barrel, put two hands on the reins guiding your horse, keeping his head under your line of sight to the first axis point, which is three to four feet to the right of the first barrel. When you reach your first axis point, you should be sitting down and dropping your outside rein if you're going to ride one-handed.

You'll look ahead to your next position three to four feet to the right of the third barrel, keeping your hands forward.

After you round the third barrel and start home, don't look at the timer or the timer line except in your peripheral vision. If you do, you'll let up before the line. Look at the end point you've already determined before the run.

The "whoa" at the end is the last transition area. Sit down, melt into your horse, tell him "whoa" and come to a smooth transition all the way to a stop.

Stop straight in the alley or against a fence in a closed arena. If you start letting the horse turn to stop, he'll begin slowing down too early. Also, it's strenuous physically on the horse to stop as he's turning because in addition to the stress of stopping, his body is twisting at the same time. However, there are horses that don't like running into closed gates, no matter what you do. Avoid those kinds of arenas if that's the case.

If you have a long alleyway, don't just slam your horse down to stop. That causes unnecessary wear and tear. If you have room, opt for a gradual stop. If your horse starts to get sore in the hocks and knows a hard stop is coming, he'll tend to slow down.

Salvaging the Third Barrel

On the left is a normal third barrel with five axis points. On the right is a third barrel with a too-wide approach. To recover, use Axis Point #3 as your first axis point and you can salvage the turn. It won't be perfect but you can likely still win money.

Third barrel problems usually start with the second barrel. It's common to have the horse "hang" a little coming off the second, and end up leaving the barrel too bent. When this happens, the horse tends to come off the barrel wide.

Another thing that happens is the rider sometimes hustles the horse, looks down and actually sends him away from the second barrel too soon – again, causing a wide departure.

If you come out of the second barrel wide, it sets your pattern so that you're coming to the third barrel also too wide. Your horse will have a tendency to drop his shoulder and you'll either hit the barrel or come so close to it that you lose time adjusting the problem because your horse has to take an extra step.

Here's an important fix for this. As you approach the third barrel wide, adjust your axis points. In other words, for your starting axis point, look to Axis Point #3 instead of Axis Point #1. This way, you won't hit the barrel. It's not ideal, but if you do this, you can likely still get a check with your run. (See "Salvaging the Third Barrel" diagram.)

The biggest thing to remember is that there are always three barrels – no matter if it's Pendleton (a 27-second pattern run on a football field) or the small pattern at the Thomas & Mack in Las Vegas. Don't get rattled – just run around three barrels.

If you see riders running a long way past the barrels and you have a free-running horse, you'll know you need to rate your horse. Also, if you have a free-running horse, try to be as close to the timer as you can before you start to keep him under control If you have a horse that rates well, ride all the way into the turn.

That's the pattern, but your work in adjusting your pattern to each particular arena should have begun long before they called your name to run. Don't forget the ground and how it might affect your run.

The ground might be really deep. Think of those runaway truck ramps for semis. The deep surface slows them down. The same thing happens to horses running in deep ground; so you'll adjust your ride accordingly, knowing that you'll likely have to push your horse a little deeper into the transition area or in the case of a free-running horse, you won't have to set as early.

Hard ground has the opposite effect – speeding things up. So you'll sit down earlier on a free-running horse because you'll need more rate to prepare for the turn on the faster surface.

TIPS

Training Young Horses

Young horses have a lot of energy and their minds are going in a hundred different directions. So, from the beginning, when I work with one, I ride in the pasture first, just walking and trotting for 20 to 30 minutes. I'm so much further ahead that way than if I just take him from the barn straight to the arena.

Teaching the Pattern

Teaching the perfect pattern depends on your doing everything the same, every time. Only when you have the perfect pattern in your head and in your muscle memory is it time to introduce it to your horse.

Focus on what you're doing, especially to correct some incorrect muscle memory. Make sure your body and hand position emulate what they'll eventually do in a run – even when you're simply walking. This attention to detail pays off later.

In the beginning, trot the horse smoothly through the pattern, slowing to a walk in the transition area, then walk around the barrel.

At Axis Point #5 where you would ask for speed in the pattern at the completion of the turn, cue your horse back to a trot.

Remember the horse doesn't have to be overbent to the inside to go around the barrels fast. This is a concept a lot of barrel racers need help with. They tend to come in with the horse flexed deep to the inside when in reality the horse can work more naturally bent in the shape of the part of the turn he's on. Remember the track around the barrel and keep his shape aligned with that.

Note: If you're unable to trot your horse in the correct pattern around the barrels, he likely needs to be more broke.

As the horse becomes more confident, you'll add speed gradually. When you do, you'll watch the horse to see that he's capable of maintaining the correct position with the added speed. Any time he's not you'll go back to a slower speed. Let him become relaxed at that pace, then try more speed later.

You'll add speed first in the straightaway, always reducing to a slower speed in the turns. Even as you go faster, reducing speed for the turns reinforces collection and rate.

Some horses appear lazy because they need to be a little more broke. More time and consistent basics help that problem. But if a horse

To avoid problems, adopt a slow and easy approach to barrel training.

is really just lazy, you might carry a whip to encourage him to be a little more aggressive. To advance at this stage, your horse needs to be to the point where you ask him to go faster or slower and he does so.

Correctness is all important. In the beginning, when you're at a slow lope, bring the horse down to a trot for the turns. Then cue for the correct lead as you move back into a lope.

The next stage is to lope to the barrels, then lope slightly slower around them. If your horse takes the wrong lead between the barrels, bring him back to a trot for the turn, then go on. Don't let him lope around the barrel in the wrong lead. Be aware that you can actually teach one to go around the barrels in the wrong lead! When he does make a mistake, correct him, but don't punish him for taking the wrong lead on the straightaway.

Don't be concerned with trying to teach flying lead changes. In barrel racing, lead changes are really the responsibility of the horse because in a run, depending on the rider for a lead change cue would be a distraction. Remember, this is not reining or dressage. It's a timed event.

If he's been taught to be on the correct lead around the barrels, being on the correct lead will come naturally as your horse begins to run faster.

When you add speed, you want your horse to accept it with confidence. Does he stay correct in his pattern? If he does, great. If he doesn't, don't slam him into the ground. Don't

become angry and leave him saddled all day and night without feed and water. And don't lope his legs off. (I've actually heard of all these things!)

The horse simply made a mistake. Go back to the speed where he can be perfect and reassure him with more repetitions before asking for more speed again.

Your goal is to build a confident horse you communicate with – one that enjoys running barrels. Your job as a trainer is to make this process challenging enough that he doesn't get bored, but not so difficult that you defeat him and he gives up.

Once the horse is able to lope a smooth pattern confidently, the scenario remains the same. Continue to increase speed in small increments on the straight parts of the pattern, always remembering to go slower in the turns than you go between the barrels.

After each speed increase, evaluate. Was the horse able to maintain a perfect pattern with the added speed? If so, let him stay at that new speed for a while, becoming comfortable with it, before asking for more. There's always a comfortable speed – one at which your horse can be perfect – and, as a trainer, you need to recognize what that speed is. Ask him to push the limits of his comfort zone, but then come back to a reassuring pace if he's not able to handle a faster run.

When the horse is relaxed with a particular speed and has consistently been able to go mistake-free at that speed, add a little more. When he's confident with that, you can add even more.

Once I've progressed to the point that the horse is running the pattern, I only make a run at top speed when I am taking him to a jackpot or exhibition. His work at home from that time on is almost all slow work.

Making Mistakes

This familiar scenario might happen to you. Your horse starts to show some real talent, and you can tell he likes the barrels. He makes all the right moves, and it's easy for him. "Wow!" you say to yourself, and start letting him go faster and faster. Actually, the horse isn't working exactly right. He's not really accepting help from you, but he's so close that you let him go on and before long you're running.

Sometimes, you can get away with this, but it's not the best approach. The horse isn't mentally ready, and you're creating problems that you'll have to fix later. Problems arise for two main reasons. One, you skipped the basics so that later, when problems surface, you have no tools to fix them. And two, the horse hasn't had enough repetitions at gradually increasing speeds to be able to keep the pattern foremost in his mind at top speed.

It's hard for a horse to be mentally ready to go at full speed in just a couple of months of barrel training. A very few are okay, but most of them can't take it day in and day out. The horse might make a couple of good runs, but he'll likely go downhill after that. It takes years, in most cases, for a horse to develop a consistent and correct barrel pattern and that's with consistent riding!

Red Flags

A better route is to be aware of "red flags" that might mean you're gaining speed too quickly or that the horse is becoming stressed by the process.

The real red flag is when the run falls apart – the horse overruns the barrel, doesn't turn or dives into the barrel. When these things happen, it's time to go back to basics. Think of the problem, then think of what's missing that caused the problem.

TIPS

Take a Break

Don't underestimate the value of giving your horse some time off. If you've been riding him hard every day for two or three months, offer him a break. If you end on a positive note and leave your horse with a consistent imprint in his mind, you can get off for a couple of weeks and you'll be amazed at how much better he'll have gotten in that time. It's almost like he trained himself.

It's likely a combination of your horse being refreshed – mentally and physically. You might never know that he was a little sore, and the rest gave his body time to heal.

Below are some red flag mistakes and the underlying problem.

- Not wanting to go into the arena. The horse has experienced too much speed or too many runs. The rider has been looking at the barrels and frustrated the horse. The rider has been rough with her hands.
- Cutting in at the first barrel. The rider has failed to instill the pattern well enough, has failed to cue correctly or doesn't give the horse time to get his hindquarters around the barrels.
- Going by the first barrel. The rider asked for too much speed before the horse is ready to handle it or failed to install the basics.
- Not finishing the second and third barrels. The rider failed to guide or looked up too soon.
- Hitting barrels. The horse doesn't understand what's expected. The rider has asked for too much speed, and the run happens faster than the horse is ready for.

The above mistakes tell you the horse isn't ready to go faster. Even some seasoned horses develop problems in the pattern. The best way to correct them is to slow down and go back to the basics.

Realize that no run is ever completely perfect. Even Michael Jordan didn't make the perfect move every time he played basketball and neither will anyone else. You're going to see riders – even at the NFR – out of position and making mistakes. The point is, if you strive toward the ideal and try to do the right thing as often as possible, you're more likely to be correct most of the time.

Seasoning a horse isn't simply hauling the animal to his first barrel races and going through difficult periods where he doesn't run well because he's nervous or distracted. Give your horse a better chance at a long-term career by looking at the process differently and begin your training early.

3

SEASONING ON THE ROAD

Barrel races are won away from home – so you need a horse that's comfortable spending time in the trailer and on the road. If you take the time to make sure your horse is familiar with, and not stressed by, life on the road, then it becomes an accepted part of his routine. When he's mentally relaxed in new surroundings, he'll stay much fresher physically.

Just because hauling is old hat to you doesn't mean it won't be strange and intimidating to a young or inexperienced horse. Part of training for a long competitive career is getting your horse comfortable with being on the road. It's a basic part of helping him learn his job.

Many would-be great barrel horses fight the trailer. Although such a horse could be a winner, the times he'll clock won't be up to speed because hauling to the barrel race made him sore enough or tired enough to lose what it takes to win. Often, such horses were frightened by trailering at a young age. They were either rushed or made uncomfortable.

Then, there are horses that run well at events close to home, but won't eat or drink well on the road. After a while, they lose weight, strength and sharpness – and that winning edge.

Learning to Haul

As you lay the foundation for a successful barrel-racing career, it only makes sense to pay attention to the hauling part of the process. Your horse will spend more time in the trailer than he will running the barrel pattern.

Trailering is an important part of basic schooling, so early on I take steps to make it a normal part of my horses' lives. I evaluate and assess the barrel prospect's progress in learning to haul just as I do any other basic skill in the program. Even in the beginning, I keep hay in the trailer when hauling. The goal is to make the trailer ride as pleasant as possible.

How you haul the horse is essential. Besides the trailer being comfortable inside – it's not too hot or cold and provides a smooth and level ride – your driving should be as smooth as possible. Steady stops and starts, careful turns and a reasonable speed all have an effect on how your horse hauls.

TIPS

Trailer Wrap

I don't normally wrap my horses to haul them in a trailer because, for the most part, it's not possible to wrap the legs tightly enough to support them anyhow. However, I might wrap to protect inexperienced horses' legs and those of horses hauling with them. It takes some time for novice horses to learn to ride in the trailer balanced, so they don't step on other horses.

If the inexperienced horse is next to one that's a known kicker, I wrap for protection. Also, if a horse has legs that tend to swell or stock up at any time, I like to wrap.

If you don't know how to wrap correctly, you can bow a horse's tendon. In many cases, wrapping causes more problems than not wrapping. Have your veterinarian show you how to wrap properly.

Ideally, I start teaching the horse to haul properly when he's been going around the barrels at home for a couple of weeks. I ride him five days a week, and, by that time, he's gotten into the mode of working every day. If the horse is relaxed at home and accustomed to having a daily job, I haul him occasionally to different arenas for his daily workout. The day it rains and my arena is too wet is a great day to haul to an indoor arena and ride there.

My objective is to get the barrel prospect used to going to other arenas at a point in his training when everything is easy. I understand that he'll want to look at everything, but I want to see that, after a time, he brings his focus back to me and what I'm asking him to do. I want him to realize that even when the surroundings change, his job doesn't. That's a mindset I want to establish so that later when I ask him to run barrels in diverse surroundings with all kinds of distractions, he'll be confident in doing his job – making his run – no matter what's going on around him. Knowing his job will be comforting and reassuring to him in an unfamiliar environment.

Remember, horses are comforted by the familiar so repetition soothes them. They're stressed with the unfamiliar and unexpected. Therefore, from the start, give your horse security by doing things the same way and surrounding him with familiar things, no matter where you go.

For most inexperienced horses, the first trips won't be a problem, but I still like to take an older horse along for company. Horses are herd animals and copy the reactions of other horses, so I make sure I choose an older horse that's quiet and relaxed with hauling.

Difference is in the Details

Throughout my seasoning process, I continue to go to different arenas with different ground, gates and fences to help my horse understand that he has a job to do in spite of those variables.

I want to take advantage of the opportunity to introduce the inexperienced horse to everything I can that will help him later. For example, even if we're only 15 minutes from home, I make a point of offering him water out of a bucket, just as I will when he starts hauling for real. It takes a little more effort, but it pays off later.

When a horse is completely comfortable with different surroundings, my next step is to take him to a jackpot. Now he sees a different

TIPS

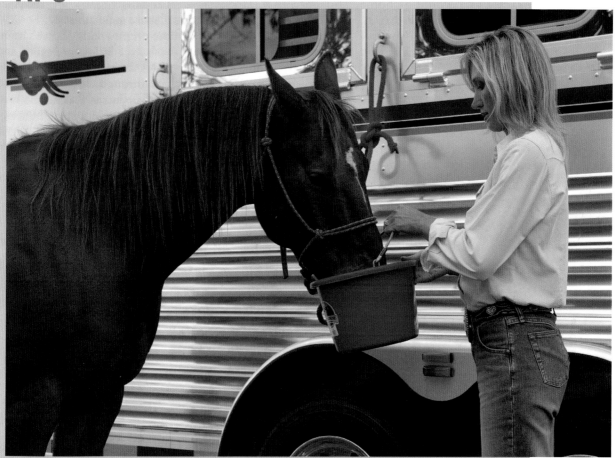

Drinks, Anyone?

When they're first going down the road, many horses won't drink. So, from the beginning, after you feed in the trailer, stop 30 minutes or an hour later and offer water. If necessary, take the horse off the trailer to walk, then offer water. You might have to hold the bucket for the horse to drink. Drinking helps prevent horses from colicking. It encourages them to keep eating, and they therefore feel better.

Cool or cold weather can cause some horses to not drink well. If you've hauled your horse all day, try to get him into a stall at night so he can eat, and you can make sure he drinks. I give electrolytes only if the horse has gotten hot and sweaty or was worked a long time.

I have horses that drink two buckets of water at night while others drink only half a bucket.

Even if you've offered your horse a drink of water at the barrel race, get in the habit of offering it again on the way home. The more you do this early on, the less problem you'll have later.

For a horse that doesn't want to eat or drink, I fill a 60cc syringe with salt water and drench his mouth. That helps make him thirsty. Don't do this with the attitude of forcing the horse to drink. Just do it gently to help him.

That's an important key to good horsemanship. Work with the horse – not against him. Don't be adversarial.

location, but with added stimuli and distractions, such as lots of other horses and the loudspeaker. The aim in those first few jackpots is to just trot him through in the exhibitions, reassure him and give him confidence.

When I arrive at the jackpot or rodeo and tie the horses to the trailer, I want the older

horse to be an example of how to stand relaxed. An inexperienced horse tied to the trailer might paw a hole in the ground, which makes his foot and shoulder ache. Hopefully, hauling him to different places and giving him a good example to follow will prevent that.

Circle M Trailers
Mabank, Texas

Once there, I saddle and do my workout exactly as I would at home. During this early stage, some horses are oblivious to their surroundings; others look at everything, spook and have trouble paying attention to their riders.

That doesn't mean one is a bad horse and another is a good horse. It doesn't mean anything. It simply lets you know that troubled one might take more time to get over being affected by his surroundings. Later in training, the nervous one that looks at everything might hunt barrels better than one that's more laid-back. Horses progress at different rates, and the polar extremes can still make good athletes.

As I go to more events and my horse's training advances, I ask for a little more speed and concentration. I trot through the pattern, then go back and lope through, so each time he goes into the arena, he learns that his job is to work barrels. I want to see him start "hunting" for them – looking to find that first barrel coming down the alley because he expects it to be there somewhere.

Throughout the seasoning process, remember to be calm and reassuring to your horse. At this stage the horse is going through a lot of stress because every new arena is unfamiliar to him. Until he learns to be comfortable with the things that don't change – you, your treatment of him, the pattern, his job – he might need a lot of attention.

Stressed Out

Throughout seasoning, whenever my horse shows signs of stress, I go back a step to something easier to let him regain his confidence. Once he's relaxed again, I ask for more.

If my horse starts to show signs of avoidance, such as not wanting to go into the arena, not listening to my cues, pulling on my hands or getting sweaty from nervousness instead of work, he's telling me he needs a break. Or maybe he starts to make mistakes in the pattern. If you know your horse, you might recognize even more subtle signs just from his body language and expression. Maybe he's swishing his tail a different way or maybe he just gets stiff. Don't overlook these things. Listen to what your horse is telling you.

Also, don't get into the trap of running your horse at full speed at home, then pushing him as fast as he can go at a jackpot. The speed plus the unfamiliar surroundings are too much for most any horse. Your horse might become afraid and insecure, and then he'll make mistakes. Definitely don't compound the problem by trying to go faster to fix the mistake.

Instead of pushing at the early jackpots, show the horse the pattern and keep him correct, always putting him into the same familiar position.

If you have problems, you can seldom fix them going at all-out speed, either at home or an event. When you're working to correct a problem, you might need to sacrifice some entry fees to rehabilitate your horse. This will be in the long-term best interest of both you and your horse.

Try to put your horse in circumstances where it's easy for him to do the right thing. Horses become more confident if you're consistent in how you cue, how you ride and how you act around them. Their security comes from getting into the arena and finding the barrels. At first, you might not have a picture-perfect run because the horse has to learn to maintain the pattern in different ground, but you'll make progress.

Experiment with how much speed you can add. If your horse is capable of a perfect pattern at a lope, lope him through the pattern at a couple of jackpots, then smooch him up into a little faster lope at the next one. If he holds together, do that same speed at the next event. If he doesn't, back down a notch to a speed he can handle, then try to bump him back up again later. The point is, only add as much speed as he's comfortable with. Do it in

TIPS

Discipline

A horse is a herd animal, used to living under certain rules, and either being the boss or having a boss in the equine pecking order. Because of this, horses don't resent discipline, as long as it's fair.

Sometimes we see barrel racers go over the line. I can't imagine beating a horse when you're training him. That just means you haven't done your job.

When a horse doesn't work right, I've often heard people say, "You can't let that horse get away with that." That's not the attitude to have. Don't get into the punishing mode and forget everything else.

For example, when a horse spooks, an unthinking rider might whip the animal up to whatever he spooked at. I've found, though, that when a horse spooks, if I just go on and don't buy into it, he generally gets over it.

And remember, if a horse makes a mistake, it's just a mistake. Correct him, and he'll learn from it and be less likely to do it again. On the other hand, if you overdo, he might associate the whole issue as something bad and have a lot of anxiety about it. Then, it'll be harder for him to learn in the future.

small increments instead of going from a lope to an all-out run in one big step.

At every stage in training a barrel horse it's absolutely essential to evaluate. That's how you'll know when to go to the next step, and what the next step is!

Failing to do so can make you go too slow for too long or go too fast too soon. Both are mistakes that can be avoided if you pay attention to the signs your horse gives you.

A lot of futurity horses get made too fast. It's not good when they're trained by the calendar instead of by their own progress. A lot is expected of them too early because of the futurity payments someone has made for them.

You can also err in the opposite direction – by letting a horse go too slowly too long. If you're still loping around the barrels after two years, that's obviously not the approach you want to take.

If the horse is doing better with each run, go on with him. The key is gradual improvement. Say the winning time is a second faster than you are. Two months later, you're consistently two or three tenths off. That's the right kind of progress. The horse improves gradually.

And the biggest thing we need as riders is patience - lots and lots of patience.

If your horse tends to be nervous, you might need to hand-walk him before the run. At best, it'll help him relax and at the very least it'll help prevent him from tiring himself before a run.

Keep the Faith

The seasoning process takes time. It's easy to get frustrated and want to hurry the process but keep in mind you're trying to create a long-term performer. I believe in my program – I've seen it work. So I have enough faith to keep it slow.

No horse is perfect, just as no rider is perfect. If you constantly pick at a horse for every little thing, you won't gain anything. For example, you might have an inexperienced horse that's having a problem going past the barrel. If you keep over-doing, you'll get him scared and panicked. Then, he'll tense up. He might actually be so tense that when he gets to the barrel, his body might not be able to shape and bend around it.

Instead of putting more pressure on him to get it right at that speed, go down a notch in speed to a pace he can handle – build his confidence. Then, when he thinks it's easy, ask him to try it faster again.

Set Goals

As your horse becomes seasoned, it's time to consider his future. Set a goal as to what you want to do with him. Is your goal to go to jackpots, turn him into a rodeo horse, sell him?

If you're content with jackpots, as long as you're winning, pick out the biggest jackpots with the most money. Beware of over-running and useless wear and tear on your horse's body. Don't waste your horse at the $20 jackpots if he can win the bigger ones.

If your goal is to turn him into a rodeo horse and he's doing well at jackpots, enter a small rodeo and when you get there, ride like you're riding at the jackpot.

That's important. A lot of people ride differently in front of a rodeo crowd, and when they do, their nervous energy and anxiousness carry over to their horses. Tell yourself that this is just another barrel race, and your job as a rider is just what it's always been. Ride calmly and consistently and reassure your horse. Don't get excited and over-ride. At the rodeo, make the same kind of run you did at the jackpots when you were winning. Accept that you might not win the rodeo, but remember your long-term goal.

Your horse might see a bull going down the alley or get distracted by the crowd or band. Do as much as you can in advance. Play music in the arena at home. If he's never seen cattle, get him used to them before the rodeo. If you have a neighbor with cattle, ask if you can ride through them so your horse doesn't see them for the first time in a scary environment. If the horse is comfortable with cattle before the rodeo, it's one less obstacle to overcome.

Remember that your horse is going through a learning curve and getting seasoned at rodeos can take a while. Don't pretend that he's been a rodeo horse for three years. Ride your horse, not your competition's horses. Stick to your game plan.

Different Strokes

Cruiser hunted his barrels at the first few rodeos I took him to, but he looked around at everything else for three years! I'd be going to the first barrel, and he'd be watching people in the grandstand. Things always caught his eye, and if I took him into the arena and let him look around, he'd find more things to spook at later.

With Scamper, it was a different story. In the beginning, he wanted to get the feel of the ground in a new arena or he wouldn't run. So, the first few years I'd go a day earlier to ride in the arena. Sometimes there are sacrifices you have to make to win. I wanted to win so I made my travel plans to get him there early. Even as he got older, he still had more confidence if he'd had a chance to get into the arena ahead of time.

How you treat your horse before a run is important, too. Cruiser would get to the rodeo and be wound up and nervous, so the quieter I kept him, the better he did. Sometimes I had to get off and hand-walk him. I was careful not to get him around other nervous horses because it rubbed off on him.

Scamper, on the other hand, did better if I kept him awake and ready to go. He needed to be a little more on his toes, so I didn't just sit on him and relax. It was best to keep him walking and moving.

Warm-up Routine

Warm-up is important from the beginning and just as I've laid other training foundations with my horse, I've created a familiar warm-up, as well. Through the months of training, the daily warm-up has become routine. Our relaxing "get it together" time includes calm walking, trotting, loping, stopping, backing and bending. All help my horse transition into the work mode loosened up, not ridden down. That familiar process helps him focus in an unfamiliar place.

What seems to work really well on an inexperienced horse is to get on him early, about the time the jackpot starts. I like to just sit and relax. I watch the barrel race, then walk around, trot and lope in the warm-up area. Then I take him back and tie him to the trailer or in the stall. I just want to give him a good experience around the arena and warm-up area.

An hour before the run, I get on and do a lot of walking. Then I go through the normal warm-up routine and just keep walking slowly right up to the time for the run. I head up the alleyway, gradually move into a trot, lope, then when I see my horse focus on the first barrel – when I see those ears perk up and acknowledge the barrel – I let him go.

At rodeos, you have to adjust to what the facility provides in the way of warm-up space. Some professional rodeos don't have a lot of space for contestants to get ready so the biggest thing is walking and flexing. At the Days of 47 Rodeo held in Salt Lake City's Delta Center, for example, there's a tiny round warm-up area where the team ropers and calf ropers warm up with you. On an experienced

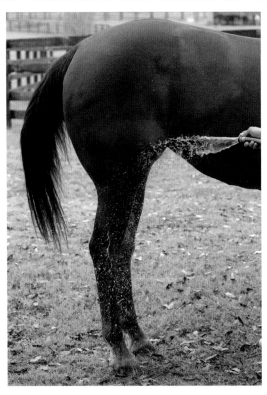

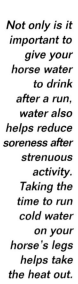

Not only is it important to give your horse water to drink after a run, water also helps reduce soreness after strenuous activity. Taking the time to run cold water on your horse's legs helps take the heat out.

After a Run

When you complete your run, get off, loosen the cinch. Pet your horse and reassure him while you take off the leg boots. Walk him back to the trailer; unsaddle and give him a drink immediately. Some horses readily drink and others won't; get to know your horse's preferences.

Cruiser was the type that if he didn't get to drink while I was unsaddling, he wouldn't drink later on. When I got back to the trailer I always had a full bucket of water waiting for him. He'd drink from a quarter to a half a bucket, but if I waited another 30 minutes, he wouldn't drink at all.

Walking your horse around after a run helps prevent him from getting sore. You'll know when you've walked enough; you can tell by his expression when he's relaxed. His respiration returns to normal. If he's been sweating, he'll have begun to dry off. He'll look calmer and more relaxed. Normally, if your horse is in shape and you warm up correctly and haven't overdone, he'll cool down fairly fast.

After a run, I run cold water on my horse's legs for about 10 minutes. If I'm not able to do that, I use pure alcohol to cool his legs, but I prefer water as it doesn't dry the skin like alcohol. Cold water helps take heat out of legs. Plus, if you do that with a green horse, you're teaching him to expect that later. Scamper enjoyed the water. He'd pop his lips in it and play.

Weather affects how you handle your warm-up and cool-down. A lot of people in cold climates haul their horses to an indoor arena. It might be 10 degrees outside and 60 inside. You've got to be careful not to let your horse get too hot. Even with your horse blanketed, there's an extreme temperature change. And if he goes outside and he's still breathing heavy, that cold air can be a shock to his lungs. Don't take your horse outside until he's completely dry.

Summarize Seasoning

In the process of seasoning your horse, you're going to go to places that are unlike anything he's ever seen before. Your treatment of the situation and of him helps determine whether he handles it well or not. For example, the first time you go to a large arena where the first barrel is a long way from the alley, don't go 100 miles per hour to the first barrel, but don't choke up on him either. Either one of those things would be different and upsetting to him. Get to the edge of the alley, let him

horse, if there's not a good place to lope and trot, stay on and walk a longer time.

Adjust your preparation based on the horse. If you've been on him for two hours and loped and loped and his head's on the ground and his time wasn't good; you know you warmed up too soon and too long.

Feed is Fuel

You also might not be feeding what your horse needs in the way of nutrition. The food you give before his run is fuel and energy for the run. The worst thing you can do is starve a nervous horse. That type is definitely better with food.

I always feed my horse a couple of hours before I run. I give a small amount of grain (about half the normal ration) and a little hay. I leave water there, but won't let him drink more than half a bucket so he won't feel too full and weighted down.

I give the second half of the grain after the run along with hay. After a run, my horse will be somewhat depleted, and I want to help him recover. Plus, eating is comforting and relaxing to him and keeps him occupied.

When you get to the barrel race and you're up in an hour, remember that the horse has been in the trailer a couple of hours. He's probably thirsty so let him at least drink a quarter of a bucket before his run. And be sure to give water afterward.

focus and spot the first barrel, then go. Ride your same position. Do everything the same.

If you've done your training properly, your horse should know that his job is to go out there and hunt barrels in a large or small arena.

Lights in a new arena can be distracting at first, but often nighttime runs tend to be better for green horses. Since they can't see outside the arena, they focus on the familiar pattern of three barrels. In the daytime they see everything, and it's easier for them to get scared or distracted.

I normally don't make any headgear adjustments for different arenas. I depend on my horse and make things familiar so I wouldn't change headgear.

Remember, consistency is very important in seasoning your horse for the long haul.

A well-seasoned horse takes time, patience and consistency.

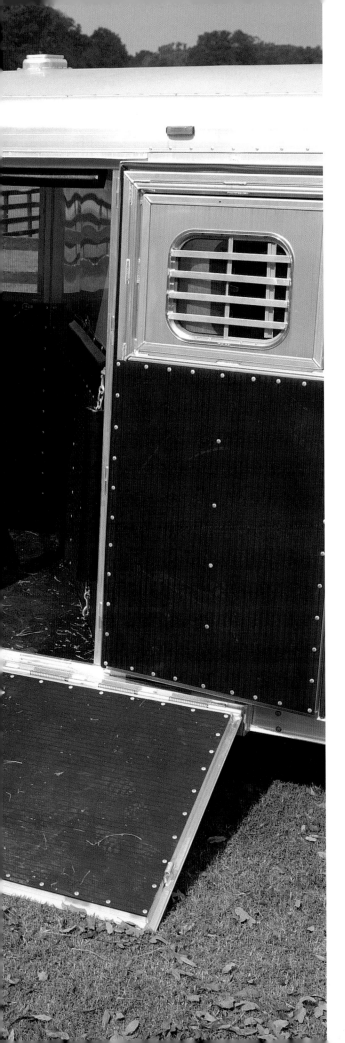

When your horse is seasoned and has proven that he's capable of winning, your job changes. Now the challenge is to keep him working, and it's not always the rider who has the best horse who wins. It sometimes comes down to who's the best competitor, who takes the best care of her horse and who's willing to do the extra things it takes to be on top.

4

THE STRATEGY OF COMPETITION

Before I go in to make a run, I basically think about my position – how I want to start and where I want to be in the alley. I concentrate on making sure that I'm not getting tense on my horse and letting him feel that. Foremost in my mind is how I'm going to guide my horse through this particular pattern.

There's seldom a perfect run or perfect ground so I know I have to be able to react to whatever happens. If I've practiced and thought about it ahead of time, and done my homework, I'll react correctly.

You have to stay on top of things if you want to win barrel races. Take responsibility for doing the things you need to do to win and don't expect others to do them for you.

Know Thy Horse

The secret to keeping a horse working well is really knowing him. Know what's comfortable to him. Know what makes him relaxed. Know his special needs. No one else is going to know your horse like you do. No one should be as familiar and comforting to him as you are. It takes time to get to know your horse. Manage your schedule so you're not just rushing through everything with him. If you just throw a saddle on him, go to the arena and work him, then put him away, you don't know him. Relax with him so he can become relaxed with you.

You can choose to focus on and spend time on shopping or visiting with your friends or you can choose to get to know your horse better. Take the extra steps, and go the extra distance to make sure your horse is comfortable and understand that what works for one horse doesn't necessarily work for another.

Just because your traveling partner's horse can haul all day and run well when it gets to a barrel race doesn't mean your horse can do the same thing. Horses are all different. If your horse doesn't handle the hauling as well, you can still win. You just have to find a schedule the horse can tolerate.

After the seasoning process, you should have a pretty good idea of what makes your horse win. You might need to get to the barrel race ahead of time and find a facility that will allow him to relax and recover from the hauling. You might need to spend more time riding him before the rodeo. It might be that you can schedule only a few events.

Study your horse. Does he get stressed when he can't see other horses? Then, make sure he can see them. You don't want stress to drain his energy or rattle him to the point that he can't perform as well.

TIPS

Don't Leave Home Without These

- Water bucket – Always make sure you have a water bucket.
- Feed – Even for a day trip, take hay and grain. You know how shaky and weak you feel when you don't eat. You sure don't want to rely on a horse that feels that way.
- First-aid kit for horse – Handy items to take include Betadine®, antibacterial ointment, vet wrap, gauze, needles and syringes. It's also a good idea to have Banamine® and "bute" (phenylbutazone) on hand in case a horse colics or gets hurt. Sometimes on the road it's hard to find a veterinarian.
- First-aid kit for rider – Keep a supply of Band-Aids, aspirin or Advil, antibacterial ointment and, if necessary, allergy medication. (I have a homeopathic medicine kit I take with me.)
- Stall fork – Be prepared to keep the trailer (and stall) clean for your horse.
- Mechanical items – Carry a jack and a lug wrench for changing tires. Don't let not having something like that cost you time and cause your horse to have to spend hours standing in a hot trailer. Pack a hazard reflector, flares, an emergency road kit, as well as wheel chocks to secure the trailer and a block to drive the trailer onto when you change a tire. Also, have some fuses, a flashlight, jumper cables and a tool kit with hammer, pliers, screwdrivers, etc.
- Security - It's not a bad idea to carry a can of pepper spray or Mace™ with you if you're ever stopped on the side of the road.
- Fix-it items – Have scissors, duct tape, WD40, leather punch and extra snaps, Conway buckles and Chicago screws.
- Extra halter – Carry an extra halter and lead in case something happens to the one you have on your horse.
- Extra bridle and bit - Pack an extra bridle, bit and reins set-up exactly like your competition bridle. You never know. You might lose your headgear, get it stolen or the reins might break. And it's often hard to find a particular bit on the road.
- Extra set of leg boots – Clean your boots in between runs, but in case they get muddy or wet during a run and you don't have time to dry them, you've got a backup set.
- Extra set of horseshoes – Definitely carry spare horseshoes. Either take a set that your shoer has taken off or have him make an extra full set. On the road you can't always find a shoer. But if you have a shoe already shaped to your horse's foot, the substitute shoer is less likely to mess your horse up.
- Shoeing tools – Have hoof-pullers in case you spring a shoe.
- Portable panels – These are a good thing if you have room in your trailer. There will be times when you can't find readily available stalls or pens. Portable panels at least allow your horse to relax, move around and put his head down.
- Extra clothes – Because you can spill something on yourself or tear something, it's always good to have an extra pair of pants and shirt. Also, even if you're just going to jackpots, keep a long-sleeve shirt and western hat in your rig. You never know when there might be a dress code.
- Blankets – Even in summertime, it can turn chilly at night. In northern climates summertime nights can be cold so take a blanket or sheets for your horse.
- Coat – Don't forget to bring a warm coat or jacket for yourself, as well as a rain coat.

There's a big difference in the trailer I started rodeoing in and the one I use now, but there are similarities, too. In the old stock trailer (left), Scamper would turn around and ride backward. The new backward slant trailer gives horses the same feel.

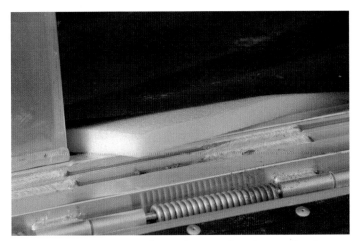

Instead of using shavings for cushioning, I prefer matting foam under the rubber mats.

Fans in the trailer help provide air circulation and keep horses cooler in hot weather.

You've seen this scenario. A horse is at a rodeo and he's jumping up and down, digging a hole by pawing at the side of the trailer, whinnying and fussing. You ask what's up with that horse, and the owner says something like, "I'm going to teach him a lesson. He doesn't like to be tied to the trailer. He needs to get used to it."

She's right, he does need to get used to it, but is this the best time and place? Since she's entered in the rodeo and going to make a run on him tonight, is she really doing him and herself the most good by allowing him to sweat and fret like that? Not only does it likely wear him out for the night's run but it also might convince him that being at a rodeo is very stressful, and he might never get over it. A better solution might be to stay with the horse, spend time with him, ride or brush him, pamper him so he can relax and have a chance at winning. Then, once she's back at home, she should take steps to familiarize him with being tied to the trailer, away from other horses.

Trailering Savvy

A horse's attitude at a barrel race depends, in large part, on how he gets there. On the way to the event, regularly stop and check your horse in the trailer to make sure he's not too cold or too warm. Open or shut the trailer windows accordingly. If you have several horses in a trailer with the windows shut, the horses will become very hot just from their own body heat. Be conscious of the weather outside so your horse doesn't overheat.

Make sure the trailer has proper ventilation and know what it feels like inside. You might have the windows open, but if you have screens on, the air flow is still restricted. I take all the screens out so the windows get better air flow through them. Every trailer's air flow is different. Figure out which windows and which vents provide the best ventilation.

Insulated roofs make a huge difference in keeping a trailer cooler in hot weather. They also keep it warmer with less condensation in cold weather. Fans are great. Even when you stop in traffic, to eat or for gas, the horses have a continuous air flow.

As far as bedding the trailer, I like to put a little shavings where the horse urinates. I don't use shavings for cushioning, though, as they can move around and ball up under the horse's feet. A better cushion is matting foam placed under the rubber mats to provide shock-absorbency. Also, shavings in the trailer – especially in the summer with the windows open – can cause dust if the air flow is right. If you see dust on the horse's back or matted in the eyes, it might be going into the horse's lungs, as well.

On a four- to five-hour trip, it's not necessary to take horses out of the trailer; but for longer trips, unload them out about halfway through. Unfortunately, when traveling, you can't always find good places to do that. One thing I discourage is pulling into a truck stop and tying the horses to the trailer while you go in and eat. Generally, the horses can't relax watching the trucks pull in and out. Worse, they could get loose. Also, it's usually not the best surface to have them stand on. Instead, keep them in the trailer, where it's safe and secure, and they can rest.

When you do stop, walk your horse around 10 to15 minutes. Of course, that depends on how much time you have as you travel from one event to the next. If you have plenty of time and the grass looks good where you're at, stay a little longer.

If you stop somewhere and the wind is about to knock you over and dirt blows into your eyes, it's not much fun for your horse or you. Try to stop in a place and at a time the horse can rest.

Be sure to carry water with you. You won't always be close to water when you stop. If you have a living-quarters trailer, make sure it has a water nozzle. If not, carry a couple of jugs of water with you.

I keep hay in the trailer most all the time. This helps eliminate the chances of your horse colicking. Water and feed are two very important things to have while traveling. Not only does your horse get his usual supply of hay

and grain, but eating also helps keep his intestines moving, thus preventing any colic problems. I use hay bags as I think they give the horses more room than mangers.

I prefer backward slant-ride trailers. When I first started hauling Scamper, I had a stock trailer, and he'd always turn around and ride backward. As he began winning and I got a better trailer, I'd put him in the front stall and let him turn around.

One year we had a bad wreck in California when a semitrailer came unhooked and we hit it from behind. If Scamper hadn't been backward so his hindquarters took the blow, we wouldn't have gotten through it as well. However, you don't have to be in a wreck for your horse to benefit from a backward ride. How many times have you had to slam on the brakes because a car pulled out in front of you? In a backward position, your horse is much more able to withstand a sudden jolt. And that way you don't take a chance on something happening to your horse's neck or knees.

As far as trailer options, air-ride suspensions make a difference in horses' comfort. They're great and Scamper would have loved them in his day.

Some horses are claustrophobic. Therefore, on all my trailers, I have divider bars so horses can see one another instead of solid walls. To me, the ideal trailer-compartment configuration would be to have one solid partition wall in case I have to haul a stallion or a horse that wants to fight. Then, the other stalls would just have bars so the other horses would feel less closed in.

Drop-down windows are also great for claustrophobic horses. If you use a mesh screen, leave one corner unbuckled.

Make sure your trailer suits your horse. For example, if you have a three-horse bumper-pull with no drop-down windows and you think your horse isn't hauling well, borrow a gooseneck trailer with drop-down windows and see if he travels better in it. If he does, you might spend the extra money to put him into a better ride.

Gooseneck trailers don't have the whipping or swaying action of bumper-pull trailers, and I feel they're more stable and safer. The quality of the trailer is very important. Obviously, you never expect to have an accident, but if you do, you want as much protection around your horses as possible. Trailers with good frames and solid walls are worth the money.

TIPS

Subtle Signs to Watch For

Horses can't talk, but they often try to let you know what's wrong. It's up to you to recognize it. Be aware if your horse does something out of character, such as:

- Refuses to go into the arena, when that's usually not a problem.
- Doesn't eat, when he usually has an appetite. Take his temperature immediately. Horses typically won't eat when running a fever.
- Paws or looks stressed.
- Seems grumpy, when he's normally laid-back.

- Has discharge from the nose. Clear discharge can be just an allergic reaction. Thicker, whitish or yellowish discharge is usually indicative of some sort of respiratory condition.
- Points a front foot, which is a sign of soreness.
- Exhibits irregular gaits – limping, head bobbing, short-stepping are signs of soreness.
- Has diarrhea or loose stools, which might indicate stress or something more serious. Check with your vet it if it persists.
- Is lethargic. If the horse seems tired or not his normal self, you might have a veterinarian check his blood count.

In the trailer or out, be aware of what your horse is feeling at all times. Is he getting too warm tied in the sun? Does he seem fretful? Is he comfortable?

Home Away from Home

When you stall your horse, take time to evaluate the facility. Look at the stall, especially if it's old or in a fairground. There might be nails where buckets or bridles were hung on the wall. If it's dark, check the stall with a flashlight. Clean it out if it hasn't been cleaned. Make sure there's no hidden trash. Remove old feed and hay.

For stalls with concrete floors, put a lot of shavings down so your horse can rest comfortably.

Listen to Your Horse

Seasonal changes affect your ability to win only if you let them. Say you've been through the winter going to small indoor pens, and when you go outdoors, your horse falls apart. Know your best bet is to go to small arenas for a while. Play to your strengths until you get the problem fixed.

That's the key to success. Chart your barrel racing plans based on what your horse tells you and on everything you're able to learn about him. Barrel racers who do this end up with better horses. Others who are clueless end up ruining theirs. What's worse is when you see someone who's winning in spite of doing everything wrong to her horse. You see a rider on the hottest horse ever, then the horse wears out and they never win again. That means she had an incredible individual that

was able to run and win regardless of what was done to him. The barrel racer looks good on that one horse; then she ruins a lot of others.

Everybody wants to do what the winner does, but all horses are different. Remember, you can't ride for the fans and the other competitors based on what they think your run should be or what they want to see. You have to be true to your horse and to what's good for him and you for the long term.

Too many runs, running your horse sore or tired or not taking care of him properly can all make a horse stop working. Know your horse's limits and yours. No one knows you and your horse like you do.

Common Mistakes

One of the biggest mistakes you can make is not giving your horse the proper nutrition as you travel down the road. The right feed helps prevent stress and keeps your horse's immune system strong. There are many infectious ailments horses can pick up on the road, so it's important that their nutritional needs are correctly met to keep their resistance high.

When on the road, I make sure I remember that horses are grazing animals, and they need something to eat most all the time. I keep hay in front of mine all the time.

Another mistake is rushing to a barrel race, thereby giving your horse a stressful trailer ride. If you're late, pull up to the arena at the last minute and run around in a hurry, you'll frighten most any horse. Not being allowed to settle in to new surroundings can scare an inexperienced horse even more than his strange, new environment. Even if you're late because you had a flat tire, don't scare your horse. Control your body language so you move quietly and slowly and don't panic. Don't get rattled. Horses feed off that. They need consistency and gain confidence if you're careful to act the same around them all the time.

Check it Out

When you arrive at the barrel race, find a program to see what time the barrel race is scheduled and ask the secretary if the posted or written information is correct. Some events add half of the bull riding before the barrel racing – that can cost 30 minutes.

Look at the arena. Check the position of the alley compared to the first barrel. In some small arenas you might find that you can't see the first barrel until you clear the alley. If you come running from the far end of the alley, you might overshoot the first barrel, so let your horse move forward in the alley but not really take off until you feel him "see" the first barrel. That tiny difference in speed gives the horse the best chance to spot the first barrel in time.

Note where the timer is in relation to the gate. If the timer is near the gate, you'd better be riding going out so you don't slow down before you cross the timer line. Also, check out the setup and make sure there's sufficient room to get your horse stopped.

Is it a big arena, with barrels out in the open or a little pen with the barrels on the fence? That determines your pattern strategy, as I discussed in Chapter 2.

Look at the ground – the type of ground and condition – whether it's wet or dry, deep or shallow.

If the barrel race takes place at a rodeo, watch some of the rough-stock events to see how the animals handle the ground. You might see some of the broncs slipping at certain spots. If you're the first barrel racer out, you'll know you need to be a little cautious in those areas. Watch, and ask girls who ran ahead of you how the ground was. You don't want to be afraid, but the most important thing is to save the horse. The big problem with rodeos is that the ground is never as good as it is at jackpots.

If the ground is bad you shouldn't just blow in there as fast as you can. Know how to help your horse slow down. With Scamper, the first few years he'd fall down when we'd get into bad ground. Over time, we finally got to where I could get to the barrels, bump lightly and say "Whoa, whoa" and he knew to stand up.

For the Record

As far as scheduling your rodeos – once your horse is seasoned and you know when and where he runs best – plan and enter based on those factors and not on just how many there are to go to.

If your horse is working well and he's not sore or showing signs of stress, enter three events in one weekend. If he runs just as well on the third run as he did the first, you can do the same thing the next weekend. But, if by the third run you notice he's not working as well or getting rattled, then schedule two for the next weekend and give him a day in between.

Continue to evaluate because things don't always stay the same. If you've been going to three races a weekend, ask yourself when your horse is at his best. If he's consistently good on first run, then not as good on the second, you know that he's getting sore from the first run or not handling the stress, or that something is happening to diminish performance.

The more you haul, the more you should learn about your horse. You also learn about facilities – everything from stalling to arena details should be recorded in your competition journal. Carefully record any information that might help you later. Then, take the time to study what you've seen. You might find that after a run on really hard ground, your horse needs a day to recover, but he can run competitively three nights in a row on soft ground.

Look for red flags. Maybe your horse has been checked by the vet and is completely sound, but you're still getting one good run and then he doesn't work. Have you checked the tree in your saddle? A broken tree can cause extreme discomfort and soreness.

A journal with notes from each event is invaluable. Write the time you ran, the time that won the barrel race and what happened during your run. Make a note if you knocked over a barrel – which one was it? Why did you hit it? Was the ground deep, shallow, shifty, sticky, slick, hard, soft, muddy? Did the ground get better on the last day? Was there a side or center alley?

Some of those things can change with Mother Nature or a new ground man, a mistakenly over-watered arena or broken equipment. All kinds of things can affect a run, but your notes will give you an advantage, both in evaluating your performance and planning your schedule for the next year.

TIPS

Charmayne's 2002 Journal

Keeping detailed records on the road pays off. You create a guide that tells you what arena conditions are like at different locations, how your horse worked there and many other variables. You'll refer to it again and again.

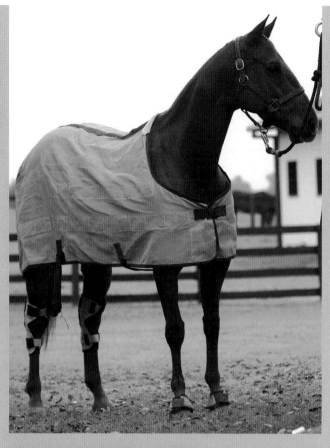

Magnetic blankets, hydrotherapy boots and sound-wave machines can all be tools in keeping your horse feeling his best.

Be sure to write down your thoughts on your own performance, as well. As a rider, I think I could've made a difference every time I competed. Be aware of what you might have done differently. What could you have done to help the horse or make the run better? Was there something different you should've done warming up? Or during the run should you have hustled more between barrels or did you over-ride. Sometimes, at the barrel race, riders see everyone going fast, and they lose sight of their game plan. They come into the arena pushing and whipping when that wasn't really what the horse needed.

Don't be afraid to analyze yourself. Often, when people say "that darn horse did this or that," it's really the rider who caused the problems. Riders often start hitting barrels when they start going to rodeos. They've lost their proper position because the competition got them excited and they went from riding the horse as a novice horse to treating it like a seasoned 15-year-old. So they kick it right past the barrel and then wonder why the horse messed up.

However, there's a limit to how much you should analyze. Don't get wrapped up in over-analyzing, either. Take everything with moderation. Don't chastise yourself for five hours each night, thinking "I should have done that." You're not going to figure something out after two weekends.

The Challenges

The challenge of barrel racing is in putting all the pieces together and developing a plan. There's no miracle or magic. Instead, it's hard work and dedication. That means adjusting little things as you go along, making changes to see if that fixes the problem. If it doesn't, don't give up. It might be something else. The easiest thing to do is be a quitter and give up.

Although you don't want to be a quitter, there's a time to quit on some horses. In spite of your ambitions for a horse, some want another career. There are some horses that go through the program and you give every chance to, but they just don't make it. Not every horse is meant to be a barrel horse. I see people with horses that hate barrel racing, but the people won't give up.

A lot of times riders are stressed by the arena setup. Such things as having to run in a side alley or run in first can really upset some barrel racers. That's usually a rider problem. It's all in your head. Visualize your pattern in your mind. You might start from a different angle but you'll use the same approach. The biggest thing to remember is that it's a race around three barrels. Go straight, turn right, go straight, turn left, go straight, turn left, go straight, then whoa. If you get distracted, you'll cause your horse to do the same thing.

Sound and Healthy

Keeping horses comfortable on the road is so important, and I rely on a variety of strategies to take out soreness and keep horses feeling well.

From the beginning, I introduce my barrel prospects to the pleasure of hydrotherapy. I try to cool down their legs by running water on them after every run. I use the hose and run cold water over them for about 15 minutes. A good leg and body brace and rubdown are also very helpful. I add the brace to warm water if it's cool out or cool water when it's hot and sponge my horse down. This really helps take the soreness out.

My favorite treatment for a chronic swelling from an old injury is a nitrofurazone wrap. Coat the area with ointment, then cover with a layer of brown paper (cut up a grocery or feed bag). Wrap with a thick bandage around the injured area. This will draw out swelling. Be careful about anything you put under a leg wrap, as too strong a product can blister quickly.

You can do a lot of good by massaging the horse's body with a rubber curry brush. Do it in an easy and reassuring way to make the procedure relaxing for your horse.

Magnet blankets are great for body soreness. They seem to help the horses after long rides in the trailer, and they also have a calming effect. For horses with sore feet, the magnet bell boots are good. I leave a magnet blanket on overnight if it's cool or put it on two to four hours ahead of a run.

I use a sound-wave machine on different acupressure points. If a horse is nervous, has swelling in a leg, or back soreness or if I have a mare with ovary problems, this machine is a favorite treatment choice. A booklet that comes with the machine tells where and how to treat. Horses love having this treatment and it puts them in a good frame of mind. Plus, it's good quality time spent with my horse.

If a horse has sore hocks, ice boots before and after the run for about 10 to 15 minutes are also very effective. The mini-whirlpool type boots are great, as well.

Earning your spurs (in this case trophy spurs) in barrel racing depends on setting realistic goals.

Laser machines work well. If your horse has had surgery, they accelerate healing. They're also great on scar tissue and on acupressure points. Again, the literature that comes with the laser explains where those points are and how to use the system.

I believe that for a horse to continue to make strenuous runs over and over, you have to work to keep him feeling well. I don't want him to be sore and associate running with pain.

I do everything I can to make my horse comfortable, but I'm very cautious with the use of drugs. If a horse is sore enough to need a lot of drugs, he's not really well enough to run anyway. On the other hand, if a horse has a chronic problem that a vet can correct with a treatment regimen, it makes sense to help keep your horse comfortable.

I want my horse to last as long as possible, and some medication in moderation can be a good thing. However, giving meds, such as "bute" (phenylbutazone) and Banamine®, as a matter of course for body soreness every weekend isn't a good idea. Try to find a chiropractor or acupuncturist who can help and stay away from depending on drugs because they're just not a long-term solution. You might find relief for the horse for a while, but finally it taxes his liver and kidneys. I believe in keeping the horse feeling his best by doing all the things I can do without having to rely on drugs.

I don't have a problem with events doing drug-testing because I don't want to encourage people to give their horses speed and other performance-enhancing drugs to make them run and stay up with horses that are winning legitimately. Those types of drugs have no place in our sport. They do enhance performance for the short-term, but deteriorate a horse's health and mind over time.

What's Your Goal?

One way to be successful at what you do is to set a goal that's realistic for your lifestyle. Wishing you could make the NFR (National Finals Rodeo) and making the NFR are two different things.

When you set a goal make sure it's attainable. If, for instance, your goal is to make it to the NFR, but you've got a horse with a limited amount of runs because of some physical problems, then that goal is unrealistic. Maybe a better goal would be to make the circuit finals, so you'd have to travel less.

I've had city kids who don't get to ride a horse very often come to me. They're overweight because they sit in the house everyday and watch television. "I'm going to be just like you. I'm going to be at the NFR one day," they say.

I don't see that happening.

On the other hand, if a girl who lives on a ranch, rides everyday, takes good care of horses says, "I'm going to make the NFR," I think she might have a chance.

Of course, there are exceptions. A city girl who works on a ranch, is extremely blessed with talent and spends a lot of time riding might also be able to make it happen.

I often see riders who buy expensive horses and big trucks and trailers even before they're winning. Just because you can buy it doesn't mean you can ride it. If you spend $200,000, then don't take care of your horse properly or don't spend enough time with him, it's not going to work for you.

One of the best things parents can tell their children is, "Do your best." Encouragement works far better than force. But parents must remember that their children have to want it. They should make them earn the privilege of going down the road and competing. A good plan would be to sit down as a family and set reachable goals. Once each goal is reached, a new goal can be set. Each goal is a stair step to a bigger one.

Parents should also monitor their children's progress and not be afraid to discipline them if necessary. For example, if a young rider lets her temper get the best of her and she jerks and whips her horse, her parents should reprimand her. They shouldn't allow the child's temper to ruin the horse or their investment.

Having a good attitude in competition is important, no matter what. If you can't have a good attitude at a barrel race, you probably shouldn't be there. Do something you enjoy. If you've gotten so serious about barrel racing that you've sucked the joy right out of it, that's wrong.

Also, be honest with yourself. If you're running 3D times (a rating system instituted by the National Barrel Horse Association), a good goal would be to win in 2D. Then, when you accomplish that goal, set a higher goal. By the way, if you can run 2D times, I think it's good to run in amateur rodeos just to get some experience under your belt.

Don't try to jump from jackpots to professional rodeos. It can be discouraging if you don't do well, so go to some amateur rodeos as a transition.

The competition at amateur rodeos isn't usually as tough as on the pro circuit. Once you've mastered winning amateur rodeos, you'll have more confidence going on to professional rodeos. Don't make the mistake of thinking it's going to be real easy, anywhere. Competition is tough, no matter how it looks from the stands.

Once you've set a goal, the second step is to plan how you're going to accomplish it. Clearly identify where you are right now, then decide how you're going to reach it. What are you going to do to reach your goal? How much will it cost? Can you afford it? What events will you have to go to?

As you begin competing, evaluate your progress along the way. Give yourself credit for improvement and, by the same token, take responsibility for things that go wrong. Sometimes, in concentrating on a goal, you might forget the basics. If you make mistakes, go back to your basics.

And remember, that even though you might not have reached your goal, you're farther ahead of where you were. You've begun. And every winner was once a beginner.

It's not just the horse that needs to be in great physical shape to win in tough competition. Riders, like horses, can be only as good as their conditioning and nutrition allow. To be a winning barrel racer, you have to take yourself seriously. Think of yourself as an athlete. Take care of your health, your diet, your fitness and they will positively impact your performance.

5

THE RIDER'S PHYSICAL RESPONSIBILITIES

In 1994, I hauled three horses on the road by myself. Toward the end of the year, I was at the bottom slot to make the National Finals Rodeo, so I was going to lots of rodeos, driving long hours and staying up late. I actually blacked out a couple of times. I didn't have a clue in the world as to why I felt bad or why I was dizzy now and then. I sure didn't want to go to the doctor.

Overall, I thought I was fine, although my back always hurt, my neck bothered me and I had regular headaches. I was 24 years old, but felt much older. I thought that's how it felt to rodeo, so I went on feeling like that for about four or five years. When I wasn't stressed or tired, I was fine. As soon as I'd get busy or tired, I would feel bad again. When you haul horses, you carry water buckets, lift sacks of feed and sleep sporadically. It all takes its toll on your body.

Good Nutrition is Vital

For help with my back, I sought out a chiropractor, who also happened to be into nutrition. She explained how sugar was bad for me, and that I should probably take vitamins to counteract what I wasn't getting in my diet. I realized she was right. I took good care of my horses, but I needed to take better care of myself, as well. I'd been eating a lot of junk food. Every time I'd stop for gas, I'd get an ice cream bar or a Little Debbie cake, juice and maybe a Coke. When I cut that out, I could tell an immediate difference.

I studied nutrition and found myself on the path to eating right. I soon realized that eating correctly made me feel better and helped me not be as sore. I started drinking noni juice. It made my headaches go away and gave me a lot more energy.

In those earlier days, I'd be sick four or five times a year with a cold or flu. After I got on a good nutritional program, the benefits to my immune system were immediately apparent because I stopped getting sick.

Everyone talks about how hard it is to eat well on the road. It was a complete lifestyle change for me, and it didn't come easy. I already knew better, but at the 2001 NFR, I had juice and a donut three mornings in a row.

A few days later I was sick and weak as I could be. I knocked down a barrel, and it probably cost me a world title. I got out of position going to the first barrel and didn't react in time like I normally would have. That's when it really clicked with me. It was my fault I got sick from eating like I did. I could have spoiled my chances to win a world championship because of the way I ate. At this point in my career, I wasn't counting on blind luck. If you've been at that level for nearly 20 years, you know you have to make your own luck, and I realized I was sabotaging myself.

When I understood how much my eating habits had cost me, I knew I wouldn't let it happen again. I had to be disciplined about what I ate. I completely changed my diet. I began drinking two glasses of chlorine-free water to start the day. I cut out white flour and sugar and began eating healthy snacks, lots of fresh vegetables and good, grass-fed organic beef.

One day out of the week, I would splurge and eat a dessert or part of one, but that was the limit to my sweets. I learned that sugar suppresses the immune system. If you're in a big crowd of people where there are different germs or viruses, you're more likely to pick up something.

Even on the road, you can find natural health-food markets that stock plenty of organic fruits and vegetables. If you have a living quarter trailers, you can supply food for yourself. It just takes some planning.

TIPS

Charmayne's Table

For breakfast, I often like cottage cheese, mixed with ground flax seed, flax seed oil and a vitamin/mineral supplement.

On the mornings I don't eat cottage cheese, I fix two or three eggs sprinkled with cheese. Eating protein like that helps build muscle and supplies energy. When you eat cereal (sugar and high-starch carbohydrates), you're hungry in an hour.

Between meals, eat vegetables or fruits, such as grapes, for your snacks. Other options are cheese or energy bars. There are a lot of snack bars these days that aren't loaded with sugar. Almonds and cashews are a great snack – not the salty ones, though.

A good lunch is a salad with a lot of vegetables in it.

For dinner, I eat some sort of meat, like a steak, with vegetables. I alternate that with fish or chicken.

I don't drink carbonated beverages or juices because of all the sugar in them. I drink milk and hot tea. Mostly, I drink water, and I'll have a glass of wine at dinner occasionally. Too much alcohol suppresses the immune system and kills brain cells.

One of the benefits of proper nutrition is you get more tuned in to your body, and you know when a food makes you feel bad.

Eating cereal or a doughnut for breakfast is nothing but eating white flour and sugar with very little nutritional content. Lunchtime sandwiches with white bread or a hamburger and French fries supply even more harmful carbohydrates, sodium and cholesterol. Then, if you follow with pasta for dinner, you've eaten mostly carbohydrates all day. Think of how many soft drinks in between or how much sweetened juice you drank. If you eat like this, you'll likely get weak and shaky some time during the day.

Instead, start out your day with good protein sources such as eggs, cheese, cottage cheese or yogurt. If you must eat at a fast food restaurant, try two orders of scrambled eggs. For lunch, order a salad. If you're at a rodeo and all they have is a hamburger, just eat the patty and veggies. If that doesn't fill you up, order another. Get full on the good stuff, not the bad stuff.

A Weighty Matter

Being overweight is probably one of the worst things that can happen to your barrel-racing career. There's a reason that racehorses are handicapped by adding weight. It makes it harder for them to run fast if they have to carry too much weight on their backs.

The weakest part of the horse is right where you sit – his back. There, he only has his spine to hold you. If you're heavy, you're going to hinder him. Also, if your legs are big, you can't grip your horse as well.

Most overweight riders I've ridden behind have balanced on their horses' reins to stay on, and those horses were completely frustrated.

If you're serious about barrel racing, assess your own physical condition just like you do that of your horse. Not being overweight helps your self-esteem, and that's an important part of winning. Having the discipline it takes to eat right is something you can take pride in. You're not like everyone else. Most people won't take the time to eat properly; they won't even check into it. Don't be like them. Be smart, eat smart.

Vitamins, Minerals and Other Good Things

I take a multivitamin made especially for women. The B-complex vitamins I take are coated so stomach acid doesn't dissolve them too soon. It's important to have quality vitamins so the body can break them down properly. There are also liquid vitamins on the market that are good. Your body can assimilate them easily.

I take a vitamin-mineral supplement. I also take additional vitamin C, and, if I start to feel sick, I really load up on the C and take echinacea. I think both help you get over it faster.

Because most everyone has had antibiotic treatment at some point, and antibiotics can kill off the good bacteria in the intestines that fight off disease, taking probiotics everyday is a good idea. They provide the good bacteria you need for a healthy digestive system.

You also need enzymes. Normally, you get them through food but when it's over-cooked or over-processed, enzymes are destroyed. It's very important to take enzymes to break down proteins and carbohydrates. Also, Omega 3, 6 and 9 are important for brain and nerve function and lysine is good for viruses and cold sores.

You might also look into colon-cleansing products at the health food store to get rid of all the toxins built up from the food you eat.

As soon as I started eating right and taking vitamins and other beneficial supplements, I began to think better. I didn't have highs and lows. I used to take a nap in the afternoon because I'd get so tired. I don't think of taking a nap now.

Study and be aware of how to best take care of your body with vitamins, minerals and natural measures. You might not live forever, but you'll feel better.

The Truth Behind Soft Drinks

One soft drink supplies more sugar than you'll ever need in a day. If you drink several cans a day, your body will try hard to filter all of it out. In the beginning, your body might handle it just fine, but by the time you reach 50 or 60, you'll be a candidate for adult-onset diabetes, high blood pressure, high cholesterol and cancer. Research tells us that much of this is caused or at least augmented by bad eating and drinking habits.

Aspartame in diet drinks is also not good for you. Many people are addicted to soft drinks. They think diet soda is okay, but some diet drinks have huge amounts of caffeine, as well.

Everyone knows there's caffeine in coffee, but they often don't realize how much is in soft drinks or iced tea. If you want coffee or tea, make sure it's decaffeinated.

Working out is beneficial mentally as well as physically. You have better self-esteem from knowing that you have the discipline to keep yourself in top physical condition.

If you're a nervous-type person and have trouble focusing on your run, caffeine adds to your nervousness and also has physical effects. It increases your heart rate and constricts your blood vessels.

One of the most important things you can do is to drink six to eight glasses of water a day to stay hydrated. You need water to make your body work properly – flush out the kidneys and rid your system of any toxins. Don't drink tap water that has chlorine, though. If the water smells terrible, don't drink it.

Working Out

A good workout program would be at least five days a week, 20 minutes a day. You can buy a Pilates videotape at any fitness store or online. If you haven't done these exercises before, start at the beginner level. Pilates strengthens your core stomach and back muscles, gets your respiration rate up and increases your blood flow. Your back becomes more flexible, plus the workouts keep muscles from becoming tight and tense so you can perform better.

Besides helping my posture, workouts helped my self-esteem. Knowing I had the discipline to work out gave me a better outlook on life. I got the jump on those who slept all morning and fed horses whenever they got around to it.

There's nothing like working out to give you a better outlook and positive attitude. If you tend to be depressed or negative, exercise is even more important for you. Not only does working out keep you fit and mentally alert, but it also makes you look better.

Your appearance says a lot about you as a person.

Walking is part of my program, as well. With Cruiser, I'd often lead him a mile first thing in the morning. Any kind of physical activity is good, plus you bond with your horse at the same time. It's good for you and also good for your horse.

With that said, this workout program is for someone who's trying to get to the top of the barrel-racing game. When I was running and competing all the time, winning was my No. 1 priority. Taking care of my horse and myself was at the top of my list. Then, taking care of my rig and taking care of business came next. It was basically a full-time job. However, if you're employed full-time or are a stay-at-home mom, you'll be really lucky if you get to workout once a day.

Drugs and Alcohol

You have choices, and I hope you choose to take the path that stays away from drugs and alcohol and running with a rough crowd. People who do drugs or drink too much aren't as sharp when they compete. They're impaired mentally and physically. I've known many people in rodeo who had incredible ability but burned themselves out.

The human body is an amazing thing, but it can tolerate drug and alcohol abuse only so long. After a while, it takes a toll on both body and mind. Some people are able to continue to compete, but later in life they pay the price. It's easy to tell those who've been burned out.

Taking drugs, drinking alcohol excessively, smoking and dipping chewing tobacco – you think it's just affecting you, but your family suffers as well. If you need motivation to do the right thing, do it for your family. Drugs and alcohol only mess up your life. They're not for winners.

For Appearance Sake

We judge others, and they judge us at face value. Does your outside appearance reflect the person you are inside? I think it's important to consider your appearance along with your horse's.

How can your appearance help your barrel racing?

For starters, a neat, well-kept appearance helps your confidence and your self-esteem. Plus, if you become successful in your barrel racing career, you'll need to have the right kind of appearance to attract a sponsor.

Stay current with the styles and trends. If your competition attire is a style from a decade ago, it's time to update.

Of course, there are extremes for everything. Your barrel racing sweat equity is always going to be more important than not having a hair out of place.

Beauty is more than skin deep. The most attractive appearance is a healthy one and being healthy isn't about who's the skinniest or who has the most perfect makeup.

To be a good barrel racer, you have to be strong mentally. You've got to think like a winner. You must know how not to beat yourself, how to protect yourself from negativity and how to maintain a winning edge. Winning is both physical and mental – for both you and your horse.

6

THE RIDER'S MENTAL RESPONSIBILITIES

The mental challenges accelerate as you haul down the road to compete. It's natural to be afraid and timid in the beginning. Learning not to worry what people think or how I looked was one of the biggest hurdles I had to overcome. In some ways, it was easier because I was young, but in other ways more difficult because all the people around me were adults.

After much success in amateur rodeos, I decided to turn pro. At the pro events I didn't ride like I was supposed to do because I was scared, shy and intimidated. Scamper felt it and didn't run.

At the Denver National Western Stock Show, I placed in a round, then knocked down a barrel. At the Scottsdale Jaycee's Parada Del Sol Rodeo in Arizona, I knocked over a barrel, again. Then I had a run fast enough to place at the Southwestern International Livestock Show Rodeo in El Paso, Texas, but again hit a barrel.

Believe in Yourself

Finally, my Dad had a talk with me. "You've spent a lot of money for motels, gas and entry fees, and you're going to have to go home if you don't start winning," were his words.

We'd gone through all I had saved from my earlier winnings, and Dad gave me that ultimatum before the San Antonio Livestock Show Rodeo.

Finally, it got through to me. I remember thinking, "Scamper and I are better than this."

At San Antonio some girls made fun of me. I had a green saddle pad and green reins and Scamper was hairy. I tried not to listen to them.

There were entry gates on each side of the arena at that rodeo, and it was each contestant's choice which gate to enter. All the pros worked out of the gate across the pen, but I felt that my horse would work better if I came out of the gate closest to the first barrel, so I did.

The point is, I finally did what I thought was best for my horse. I came out of my shell and rode to my potential. I rode like I'd been riding at the amateur rodeos and we won the rodeo. We didn't have to go home!

The feeling that came over me was relief. I thought to myself, "That's what I know how to

Charmayne and Scamper had been winning amateur rodeos, but when they started going to the professional rodeos there was a period of adjustment.

Winning the Houston Livestock Show PRCA Rodeo was the early highlight of Charmayne's 1984 rookie season.

PHOTO BY SPRINGER

do!" It worked because I believed in myself and in my horse.

People weren't always kind and remembering that always makes me try to be nice to newcomers to the sport. I had people tell me Scamper would win even if I rode him backward. None of them knew how much time I spent riding – how close a bond I had with Scamper.

That's where my confidence came in and not letting what people said affect me. My strength was my bond with Scamper.

My mother helped me so much. I could've been the ugliest kid in the world, and she would've told me I was pretty. When I made mistakes, she let me know, but she was always there to say, "You can do it. You're the best!" She said that to all us kids. In everything we did, her encouragement to us was never-ending.

My parents, Charlie and Gloria James, were a large part of my success. They helped me so much with their laid-back attitude. They never panicked over any situation. Mom was a rodeo queen who rode horses but never competed. I grew up in Dad's feedlot.

Along Came Scamper

Scamper hurt himself at Josey's Barrel Race the year following our win at San Antonio. He came out of the arena dragging his hind leg. He'd strained a ligament in his stifle. My first thought was, "It's okay, Scamper. We'll get you fixed."

If something happens to your horse, it's your responsibility to put his needs first, instead of being worried about yourself and the runs you might miss. Taking care of your horse is a better use of time in a crisis than wasting it on emotion and hysterics.

We bought a hand-held ultrasound machine to use on Scamper's injury. He didn't like being touched by this strange machine, so we had to rub the ultrasound machine in horse

PHOTO BY SPRINGER

There was a pot of gold at the end of the first-year rainbow as Charmayne and Scamper won the National Finals Rodeo.

Charmayne and Scamper both smile at winning their first Women's Professional Rodeo Association World Championship in 1984 in Oklahoma City, Oklahoma.

Take advantage of good advice so that success and the physical proof of it will come to you, like this commemorative bronze Charmayne received upon Scamper's induction into the ProRodeo Hall of Fame.

manure before he'd let us get near him with it because the new smell bothered him. I also ran cold water on his leg three times a day. In situations like this, you do what you have to do.

We were out of competition for two months, but my attitude was that I didn't care if I ever competed again. I just wanted Scamper to be all right. I'd already been through losing a horse that I loved.

Bardo, the horse I had before Scamper, belonged to my oldest sister, Eugenie and, when she got married, she gave him to me. He was barn sour, plus he had come off the track and would run sideways.

I rode from sunup to sundown that summer and ended up winning over $20,000 on him in amateur rodeos. One day my sister Bernadette borrowed him to make a practice run on poles. He took a bad step and shattered his front leg.

My parents searched for a new horse for me, and that's how I ended up with Scamper. (Read more about Scamper in Chapter 12, "The Horses.")

Sound Advice

There's a lot to be learned from other people – good and bad. Don't be afraid to watch what people do and incorporate some of it into your program, but also don't be afraid to do your own thing. You know your horse, so have confidence that you know what's best for him.

Not all advice is sound. Sometimes a rider gets lucky. She gets a great horse that literally trains himself and wants to stay honest. Because she wins other riders tend to follow what she does, but it might not work at all well for you and your horse.

Advice from a neighbor, a team roper or a mother who sits in the stands and has never been on a barrel horse might sometimes be well-intentioned, but it can be dead wrong.

Your best bet is to get help from people who've been successful over the years. Success isn't about winning one barrel race. It's not about getting lucky for two years in a row. It's about winning consistently year after year. Be careful what you try; there are no shortcuts. Hard work is all about being consistent and patient and riding your horse every day.

Sometimes your friends and loved ones can wreck you. That's why it's so important to know your horse so you can be your own best judge.

For example, someone makes a run. When she comes out of the arena, other barrel racers tell her what she did wrong. Some people would rather see you fail than do well. When people talk to you, listen to what they say and store it in your brain but don't accept it as the truth. Consider it to see if it has any merit. Discard it if it doesn't. Don't dwell on it.

All Work and No Play

Winning barrel races really depends on you and how hard you want to work at it. You can make a few adjustments but don't expect to win if you're not putting a hundred percent or more into it. Excuses are fine to tell other people but don't lie to yourself. Don't try to get yourself motivated before the event if you've spent more time in front of the television than with your horse for the past week.

There's no substitute for dedication and a solid work ethic. But even if you're working hard, you still need a positive mental attitude to compete. What will really help you most is knowing that you rode your horse, fed your horse, took care of his comfort and did everything to make him ready to compete. That's what will help build your confidence.

Controlling these factors will give you a better chance of winning, but there's no guarantee.

If you're working hard and still not performing up to the level you should, then you have to figure out what's going wrong. You might be riding two hours a day, but if you're practicing wrong, looking at the barrel and not maintaining your position, you're perfecting your mistakes.

Ask yourself these questions. Are you correct in your hands, body position and in where you're looking? Are you riding wisely in practice and competition or are you wrecking your horse mentally by applying too much pressure and not giving him enough relaxation? Do you need to be more in tune with your horse? Start figuring things out. Study everything that has to do with your barrel racing. Make notes about your daily riding schedule, your runs and different arenas, even weather changes.

Pilot Error

If spending 30 extra minutes a day would make you one tenth faster, would you do it? I did.

Some riders make excuses like the ground wasn't good or the conditions weren't right. They won't correct their failure to win because they won't take responsibility for the problem.

Every mistake a horse makes around a barrel is caused by the rider. Either the rider didn't teach the horse in a way he could understand, she rushed him, she didn't correct a small error before it escalated or she rode wrong (such as looking at the barrels or the fence).

I've always regarded myself as the leader in a partnership with my horse, so I hold myself accountable. Every time I make a mistake in a run, I look for ways to improve myself. I wonder, could I have warmed up my horse differently, prepared more or ridden better? Was my horse sore and I didn't pick up on it? What could I have done to improve?

Some barrel racers hit barrel after barrel. They talk about their horses, "He's a barrel hitter. He likes to hit barrels." I've never turned a horse out in the arena at home and had him hit a barrel. Horses do what we cue them to do. If we correct our signals, we can correct the problem.

It's easy to blame the horse. I've seen barrel racers come out of the arena, jerking on the bridle and hitting the horse, muttering, "He'd better figure this out."

I'm a human and I'm watching and I can't figure out what the rider wants at that point, so how can the horse? Never let your disappointment erupt into anger. If you're angry at yourself or at your horse, don't take it out on the horse. Take some time, think about it, then find a way to communicate more clearly with the horse.

Muscle Memory

Sometimes you identify a problem, work at it a week, then go to the barrel race and make the exact same mistake. Even if you know it in your head, it's hard to react automatically in a new way. Corrections have to become ingrained so that when your adrenalin is high and you have a big case of nerves, you still react in the new way, instead of reverting to the old habit. Count on at least three weeks of daily practice to change something about how you ride in a run without having to concentrate on it. Muscle memory will eventually work in your favor, and you'll automatically do the new correct thing. However, in the meantime, it's important to work on changing the ingrained habit.

What Competition Feels Like

When the announcer calls your name, does your body react with varying amounts of butterflies and adrenalin? To win, learn to welcome this feeling.

The plaque Charmayne received upon winning her 11th Women's Professional Rodeo Association world championship describes her thoughts on becoming a winner.

79

In barrel racing, your one and only job is to run the barrels.

We've all heard stories about people involved in car wrecks who literally picked up a car to save someone. They certainly didn't have super-human strength under ordinary circumstances, but their fear sent adrenalin coursing through their system to give them a short-term boost.

Ultimately you want to learn to use adrenalin-created sharpness, extra strength and quicker reactions to your advantage in competition. However, in the beginning, those feelings can be very distracting if you're already a nervous rider. All of a sudden your leg might be shaking or you might have the feeling that your stirrups, which were fine a minute ago, are uneven.

Eventually you'll feel the adrenalin hit, and it will simply mean that you're close to the run. Once you accept that this is what competition feels like – adrenalin can be your friend.

Sometimes you'll make the run and come out afterward not knowing what happened. You won't be able to remember anything! The first thing you need to do is to learn to relax so you don't black out. Think about what makes you nervous so you can rationalize and get over it. Ask yourself, "Am I afraid of the speed? The people watching?"

Tell yourself, "Yes, I can ride my horse that fast so I really don't need to be afraid. Those intimidating people aren't the ones who know me and help me do this. I don't owe them anything."

It's important to realize that you don't have to deal with just your excitement and nerves. You also have to monitor what you're transmitting to your horse. If you tighten up, your horse will, as well. If you begin to tremble, your horse is going to feel more nervous. If you stop breathing normally, your horse will too. Take some deep, relaxing breaths, sink into the saddle and think about what you're going to do in the run. Concentrate on the task at hand.

Like you, your horse gets a shot of adrenalin at the beginning of the run. That's part of what makes the second and third barrels different. The horse generally gets more speed going to the first barrel because it's usually a longer distance and it's also the beginning of his adrenalin surge. By the time he heads to the second barrel, there's a shorter distance to travel and the big adrenalin rush has faded.

Just Do Your Job

If you have the ability and the horse, but are so overcome by nervousness when it's time to compete you'll defeat yourself. Think about why you're nervous when you get to the rodeo. To counteract this, use visualization techniques in your daily practice at home. Imagine that there are people watching you, bulls in the chute, the announcer calling you, things like that. When you get to the rodeo you've already visualized everything so you're prepared.

Another way to get over this is to ride in front of people. Have people come over to your arena and watch you ride. Do what you have to do to get to the point where you can do your job.

What is your job? "To win the barrel race?"
No!

Thinking that way can trip you up. Michael Jordan was a great basketball player and, in the playoffs on national television with the game tied and seconds on the clock, his teammates always threw him the ball.

When he caught it with a second left, what was his job at that point?
"To win the game?"
No!

His job was to shoot the ball. He devoted his life to being the best. He paid for it with sweat equity. He worked at it. For him, there was a good chance that the ball would go in, and he'd win the game. But his job wasn't to worry about the outcome. It was simply to shoot the ball.

Your job, at the rodeo or the jackpot, is to run your best pattern. You might make your best run ever, setting an arena record. Then, the next person who comes in could break your record. Does that make your accomplishment any less impressive? Of course not, especially if you did the best you could on the horse you had on that day!

Just shoot the ball.

Winning and Losing

I'm often asked why I win. There are a lot of reasons. However, the number one is my love for my horses. I can't wait to see how my hard work pays off, knowing that I'm going to reap the rewards for it later.

Winning is not about having the right bit, the right saddle, a bunch of money, the fanciest trailer, the fastest horse. Often the people who win the parking lot contest aren't the ones who win the barrel race.

Winning is about being consistent, thinking positively, staying focused and taking care of business.

I also think I win because my horses like me, and they like doing their job for me. I don't want to win to impress people.

You're going to have periods where you don't win, where it's not going right, where people look down on you.

When I retired Scamper and started riding Magic, I didn't win like I did on Scamper. I'd get one good run out of 10. I knew that. I didn't need anyone to tell me. But all the while I thought of ways to improve my riding, and, in the end, Magic wasn't a world champion horse but I was able to make it to the National Finals Rodeo with him.

Simply, you don't owe anyone anything, except, of course, your parents or spouse who help you. No one else matters. The intimidating people who happen to come to the event are likely not even noticing you that much.

I'd hate to think that at a rodeo, if I didn't win, I had to go out into the stands and apologize to everyone.

I know in my heart that I did the best I could on that day, on that horse, in that arena. Sometimes that's good enough to win; sometimes it isn't. You shouldn't have to apologize, ever, for doing your best.

You'll make mistakes but you'll learn from them. At the point when you mess up in public, don't make excuses for yourself. Don't lie to yourself, saying it was the arena or the ground. Think of what you might have done at that point to change it. All barrel races are run on different ground and have different circumstances you'll have to deal with. Your job is to recognize the factors that can influence your run and figure out a way to work around them. If you do, you can win.

Act Like a Winner

On days when you don't win, act like you're on top. I always want to be the first to congratulate the winner. Barrel racing and winning don't last forever, but you can always be a good person.

When you do win, don't be a rude winner. That's the one who, when you congratulate her, says something like, "My horse didn't work well. I could've been faster." To top it all, she looks bored or grumpy. She might think she's being cool, but in reality she's insulting you. After all, she just beat you, and you were classy enough to congratulate her. Instead of graciously accepting your kind words, she misses the point. If you win, for heavens sake, enjoy it.

If you cop an attitude of "better than everyone else," you're going to get beat. At any moment something can go wrong, and you're no different than anyone else.

Courage under Fire

What can wreck you? Having a traveling partner who runs you down and makes you feel insecure about yourself is one common problem. Or, you hear the ground is bad, or someone makes a scalding run that everyone thinks no one can touch. Or it rains for your performance so you run in mud when others got a dry pen? All of this will happen to you at some

TIPS

Give Yourself A Mental Edge

Here are a few things you can do to stay mentally sharp.

- Listen to upbeat music. It can make a difference in the way you feel. It helps by getting you fired up. If you listen to sad songs that talk about cheating or someone leaving or dying, you might get the opposite effect.
- Surround yourself with positive people and stay away from the negative ones. You don't have to be rude; just say "Hi" and go on about your way.
- Don't let things that are out of your control determine your ability to win. Some things are a condition of competing or a condition of life, such as having to run down a long ramp to enter the arena, or a grouchy gate man when you come in, or not getting a good parking spot, or someone who stole your boyfriend two years ago is there and you never win when she comes to a rodeo. Those things really don't affect your run unless you let them.

point in your barrel racing career, and you'll learn whether you're steady under pressure.

I know one world champion roper, who, when he's broke, he wins big. He's almost impossible to beat if he needs the money. For other people, that kind of pressure would be too much. If they got that desperate, they couldn't do anything right.

For some riders, when they have to win, when the stakes are high, they do more. When I was a kid, my parents said if I didn't win, we couldn't keep going. My family sacrificed for my Mom to take me down the road. I knew and understood that from the beginning. Knowing those consequences made me a better person and a better competitor. It was character-building. I learned that there are consequences for not winning. Certain types of pressure are good. That's what winning is all about.

Make Your Own Luck

It's often been said that you make your own luck. You do to a certain extent. You have the opportunity to do everything you need to do with your horse if your heart is in it. If it is, you don't mind riding your horse, rubbing his legs, running water on them, working him, hand-walking him so he can eat some grass on the road, taking him to the vet – or just doing whatever makes him feel better and work better. When you ride into the arena, you know in your heart whether you have a real chance of winning and whether you deserve to win.

A tiny detail might make all the difference between winning and losing. You can hope to have luck on your side or you can make your own luck. Since barrel racing is a timed event (there could be a tenth of a second separating first to seventh place), my thinking is that if there's one thing that could make the slightest difference, do it.

Some of the things involved in making your own luck are: confidence, a bond with your horse, good hands and seat, the ability to communicate with your horse, the ability to recognize problems as they arise, a thinking approach, discipline and the ability to block outside influences.

If you're strapped for money by the time you get to the barrel race and your horse hasn't done anything for three weeks, at that point you're gambling on Lady Luck. Maybe three sevens will roll up on the slot machine, if you're lucky. The picture changes for the better if you've worked to put your horse back together, and he's on the road to recovery. Then, he has a good chance of making a competitive run. How prepared you are determines whether you're asking for luck or a chance.

Confidence is the Name of the Game

What makes a winner? Many people would answer that question by saying, "Winning, of course."

So what makes a loser? "Losing," would be their response.

So the more you lose, the bigger loser you are? "Yes," they say.

"No!" I say.

I've lost plenty of barrel races, but I'm a winner. On most of those non-winning runs, I was still a winner (even though no one else knew it) because I accomplished my goal for that day on that horse. Being a winner means being strong in your beliefs and strong in what you know and not letting other people get to you.

Confidence comes from winning, but before that it comes from taking pride in yourself and being a partner with your horse. The thing that gave me confidence in the beginning was my parents' belief in me. Also, I loved my horse so much. He was my buddy, and I knew he'd do his best for me. My horse gave me confidence, and the reason he did is that I'd spent the time with him it took to gain his confidence.

To run world class barrel times, your job is helping to guide and position your horse. You never want to be indecisive and unsure of yourself because it's not just you who'll be affected. Your horse will pick up on your insecurity and become unsure himself. If you're a confident leader, your horse will take you where you want to go – right to those gold buckles.

Buying a finished horse and buying a prospect are two very different tasks. With one, you're looking for a horse that seems to have all the attributes to succeed. With the other you're looking for a horse that has already proven he can stop the clock in the arenas you want to run. The key to success in shopping for either is knowing what you're looking for, what's acceptable and what's not. Be prepared by having your priorities in line. It's not about the prettiest horse or even the fastest horse. It's about picking the horse that suits you best.

7

THE RIGHT HORSE

When buying a horse, decide, first of all, where you want to compete – jackpots, amateur rodeos, college rodeos or the pro circuits. You should also be honest about your riding skills. If you're riding at a 3D level, you're probably not ready for a pro-rodeo horse.

Before you even look at a horse, decide how much money you can spend, then look at horses in that price range. It's probably a good idea to look at more than one if you're shopping for the first time. Once you've purchased several horses, you'll have enough experience under your belt and a feel for how horses compare to the ideal that you'll be able to see one and know whether you want to buy him.

You'll also learn by just getting out and talking to people. That doesn't mean that what everyone says is correct. Even reliable sources might not know everything about a horse, so the more you can educate yourself, the better buyer you'll become. Trying out horses is educational and because you get to ride other horses, it's also an opportunity to learn what a good horse feels like.

A girl at one of my clinics said she bought a finished horse. I could tell by riding him that he was green, because he was barely able to lope a pattern. I asked her how much she paid and she said "$3,500." That's about what you pay for a prospect, and that's what she got. Be realistic. Barrel horses have gotten more expensive in recent years.

There are some good deals to be found, but, in most cases, if you find a rodeo horse for half the going rate, you're probably buying someone's messed up horse that needs fixing.

Shop for a horse from someone reliable, but, at the same time, beware. Someone who sells horses for a living might lean more toward selling the horse than protecting the buyer.

When I shop for a horse, I don't rely on the seller to tell me things. If they do represent the horse absolutely correctly, it's a bonus.

If you're an inexperienced buyer, take someone with you but make sure he or she is a good friend who'll watch out for your best interests. You want someone who's objective and positive.

If you can, observe prospects in the pasture. Not only can you watch them move, but you also get to see how they interact with other horses. You'll get an idea of their personality and attitude as well as physical ability.

The Barrel Horse Prospect

Buying a prospect isn't as difficult as buying a finished barrel horse, but it's still a challenge. Your job is to find a horse that has the physical attributes and mental capabilities to become a barrel horse.

You have to consider budget and your time. Ask yourself how much money can you spend and where do you want this horse to take you. Set a budget, and look for horses priced within that budget.

Consider your schedule. If you're working a job and unavailable from 7:00 a.m. to 5:30 p.m. every day, is an unbroken two-year-old really the best bet just because you can save $2,000 over the price of a four-year-old that's already patterned or broke to saddle?

Good Conformation a Must

Barrel racing is one of the most physically demanding events on horses, so you want to start out with a horse that's likely to be able to take the wear and tear. Look first for good conformation. You want a body in proportion to the legs and head.

Good feet and legs are essential. I admit that I've seen a lot of good crooked-legged barrel horses, but that type conformation makes it harder on the horse and is always prone to problems. Think of how a crooked legged horse ties in at the joints. Instead of weight bearing down on two flat surfaces in the fetlock, for example, the crooked angle makes the weight bear down on one side of the joint or the other. That sets up the likelihood of problems later.

When a horse's conformation makes it difficult for him to perform the way you want, the horse is going to stay sore and his mental outlook might be sour because he'll be tired of hurting all the time.

People thought for years that long backs were bad, but I've seen that this can create a longer stride. If the rest of the horse looks good, then the long back shouldn't be a problem.

Also rule out a prospect with obvious blemishes. Wind puffs, splints and the like are warning signs in a horse that hasn't been used hard. If the horse is showing those signs of wear before training, then schooling and subsequent runs will be especially hard on him. Remember, whatever conditions you accept, you're going to have to live with.

It hurts to buy a great prospect off the racetrack and find he's already got soundness issues, but that's often the case. It's hard to be brutal in the selection process because you'll like a lot about the horse and want to ignore the rest.

There are always exceptions to rules. There are some great horses that have big hearts and great minds so they're able to overcome physical problems. However, it makes sense to start out with as few problems as possible.

Male Versus Female

I had one mare, Glancy, that was a successfully rodeo horse. As much as I liked her, I've always preferred geldings more than mares because of the hormonal changes that can bother a mare. Most of my success has come on geldings that are naturally steadier. I've also found that when I must take corrections during the training process, geldings seem to be more forgiving.

Traveling with geldings is also easier than mares and stallions. You won't need special accommodations because a gelding is fine stalled next to other horses.

Some people shy away from mares as performance horses, but if a mare is a winner, I think she's worth a little extra work.

In my experience, however, mares can be unforgiving. Some don't do as well being pushed or disciplined. I also think they tend to hold a grudge longer than geldings. And, hormonal changes can be a real factor in their day-to-day behavior, especially when they're young.

When evaluating a mare as a potential sale prospect, have your vet check her ability to reproduce, even though you're not planning to breed her. If you do decide to breed, you'll know if she can conceive. If not, you've ruled out any conditions that could affect performance.

Some mares are worse than others when they're in heat. Help manage that by having the mare cycling properly and not being overstressed.

The traditional thinking has been that when you had a mare with reproductive cycling problems (always in heat) that if you bred her, often times it would regulate the cycles and balance them out. Some of my friends have had mares with problems that came back much better after they had a foal.

By their nature, stallions are obviously going to be more aggressive than mares and geldings. Their instincts demand that they be very aware of what's going on around them. This can be detrimental if you need the horse to concentrate on the task at hand, namely running barrels.

Typically, stallions are strong and have a lot of try, which is helpful on long, hard road trips and with difficult competition schedules. But they also have a protective territorial nature, which can get in the way. Some people believe you have to be mean to stallions to gain their respect, but it's just the opposite. You have to treat them very well, and they have to trust you. However, you must be the alpha horse with them and be very diligent with boundaries. You can't let things slide and expect them not to take advantage.

With mares or stallions, be aware of housing, tying and proximity to other horses. Some mares have a tendency to kick, and stallions tend to nip, bite and be aggressive.

Breed Preferences

When shopping for a prospect, don't buy whatever is available. Your odds are better if you stick to a horse with the speed and ability to do what you want. There are exceptions, of course, but for the most part, if you buy a horse from a family noted for its good barrel horses, he'll have more likelihood of success.

I like some Thoroughbred or race breeding in my prospects. Thoroughbreds or race-bred Quarter Horses seem to have larger joints than typical, cow-bred Quarter Horses. To me, it makes sense that having larger joint space makes the horse less susceptible to cartilage damage.

For the most part, I have tried to stay away from straight cutting-bred horses. For me, they're really "feely" (sensitive) and handle great, plus they're intelligent so they train fast. However, they can give you a false sense of speed because they're so quick and athletic. Also, for the most part, they don't have the stride it takes to run and stop the clock. Some of them can be so sensitive that they're not very forgiving for barrel racers. Crossing them with running horses helps with lung capacity and stride, as well as larger joints.

There are great barrel horses bred every way, but some stallions are recognized for their barrel racing get. Personally, my two favorite bloodlines are Streaking Six

TIPS

Charmayne's Breeding Program

Black Dash is by Streakin Six, out of Patti Dash, a mare with a 111 speed index and who won nearly $70,000.

A Black Feature is by Frosty Feature, a son of Truckle Feature and out of Miss Toady Jack.

Always Sixes is by Streakin Six and out of Always Elegant, a daughter of Raise Your Glass.

Here are Charmayne's two favorite bloodlines for barrel horses.

Streakin Six – The get of Streakin Six have proven that they're ideal for running barrels. They have the conformation, speed and mind, plus horses of this bloodline seem to be forgiving.

I first fell in love with Six Fortunes, a son of Streakin Six that was a world champion racehorse. His temperament was great and he was beautiful. I bought Cruiser (son of Streakin Six out of a Masterhand-Lady Bugs Moon-bred mare) and he became a world champion. He loved running barrels.

I stand two Streakin Six sons – Black Dash and Always Sixes – and I raise my own prospects by them. Both stallions are typical sons of Streakin Six, with great minds and built-to-last conformation.

Truckle Feature – I like riding horses by Truckle Feature. I've seen a lot of nice barrel horses bred that way and I like their physical and mental toughness.

My stallion, A Black Feature, is a grandson of Truckle Feature out of a really good calf-roping mare that traces to the foundation sire Two Eyed Jack. He's incredibly smart and was still a stallion when I bought him as a two-year-old. I thought he was too good to cut. His mind was great and he was easy to ride and train, so I kept him a stallion. I thought he'd be a nice cross on my appendix Quarter Horse mares. He's forgiving and many of his foals can take a little more pressure than the average racehorse.

This filly by A Black Feature is well-balanced, even as a two-year-old.

This two-year-old gelding by Ima Too Cool and out of Frosty Feature mare is a good prospect because he's strong, well-muscled and has good bone.

and Truckle Feature, both champion Quarter Horse racehorses and outstanding sires of racehorses.

For my own breeding program, I've selected individuals that are from proven families, and they're already successful. My own stallions are Black Dash, A Black Feature and Always Sixes.

Evaluate the Prospect

After you watch the prospect, ride him, if he's broke. Some horses move like well-oiled sports cars and others are more like rickety farm trucks. Feel the difference.

If the horse isn't broke yet, watch him move in the arena or pasture. What you're looking for is a horse that runs with his feet low to the ground. He's efficient in his movement. One that looks like he climbs in front will normally not stop the clock. He spends too much time in the air. Notice if he keeps his hind legs under him running and playing. If he has the ability to lift and support his front end, he can be athletic around the barrels. You want a horse that looks like it's easy for him to move, one that's quick and agile, not clumsy. You want the athlete!

Look for a horse with a bright eye and one who'll interact with you. Get a feel for the horse's personality. In barrel racing many great horses are "alpha" horses. Such a horse is boss in the herd. He's usually a little more aggressive and has a mind of his own. That increases your challenge as a trainer because this type horse is generally more difficult to read and train and keep going. The alpha horse is also the one that, if over-handled or over-disciplined, can blow up.

As much as possible, assess the handling the horse has gotten. It should be a dealbreaker if the horse has learned wrong things or been abused. You have to spend time fixing problems and getting his trust and confidence back. That's time you could be training him. An abused horse usually has a disappointed or dull look to him. When you enter his stall, he usually turns away. These are signs that this horse has some problems, and you should look for a better partner. This part is hard for me because I want to buy them and make their lives better, and I admit I've done just that. But if I had to pick just one prospect, I would

have to pass on this type horse because some never completely overcome that initial abuse.

In riding or watching the horse move, look for any inconsistencies in length of stride, head bob, etc. Always look at a trot because problems will show up more clearly at a trot.

Even if no unsoundness shows up, but it's a strain for him to move quickly, he's probably not the one.

If the horse is broke, the best prospect is one that knows his leads, stops readily, breaks or flexes at the poll and backs. If he's not been around the barrels, make sure he can hold his leads in front and back in small and large circles.

If he's been started on barrels, his skills should be commensurate with the barrel-training time he's had. If he's been worked on barrels for six months and still can't lope a pretty smooth pattern while keeping his leads, pass on him.

A Good Fit

There's the matter of "fit." You need to be able to get along with the horse the first day you get on him. If you can't, then don't buy him because it's probably not a good fit. You'll end up fighting with him, and that handicaps your chance of ever succeeding from the very beginning.

When buying a horse, find out who trained him and how they cued him. Watch the current rider's hand and body position so you'll

TIPS

Checklist for Prospects

Here's a list of good and bad qualities to look for when shopping for a prospect.

Good Qualities
- Good Conformation
- Sound
- Good Movement
- Good Attitude
- History of good health care
- History of good handling and training
- Affordable price

Bad Qualities
- Crooked legs.
- Any unsoundness or soreness.
- Excessive blemishes for the horse's stage of life.
- Old injuries or swelling that interfere with flexion or movement. On the other hand, a horse might have an old scar that's healed properly and is simply a blemish.

- Small feet. So much rides (literally) on a barrel horse's feet, and small feet usually become a problem.
- Bad feet. If you don't know what's bad or good, ask your farrier.
- Incorrect movement. Look at the way the horse moves. Watch him walk on a hard surface with someone leading him. Make sure the horse hits the ground evenly and flatly with his feet. Some horses pick up the foot and curl so they're prone to hitting the sesamoid bones.
- Too straight hind legs. No power in the hindquarters.
- Problems with the pattern. If the horse already has problems, you don't want to start out un-training.

Cruiser has good legs and feet. He's a little long in the back, but that probably increased the length of his stride.

Even at the age of 28, Scamper still shows the balance and strength that made him such a tremendous athlete.

know what he or she did and won't confuse your new horse. It'll help you as you go on to know how to communicate with him.

If you're diligent in shopping, you'll find a prospect for which you have every expectation of success. During the training, though, you have to continue to evaluate him. Let the horse determine his career. Not every horse is destined to be a barrel horse, even if that's what you have planned for him.

It would be sad to be pushed to be a world-class athlete if you didn't have it in you, but that happens to both horses and people. People, though, come up through the ranks and are eventually eliminated at whatever level they get to. Horses just keep getting pushed. "He's doing well but not stopping the clock, so let's buzz him here or give him this or that," says the non-thinking and ill-informed rider.

Ultimately, knowing everything you can know about the horse as you go through the training process will tell you whether he has the capabilities for what you want him to do or not. You'll also be able to recognize if he's hurt or holding back for some other reason.

And again, it might just be that he's reached his peak before he gets to the level you want. Sometimes, you have to accept that and temper your dreams with reality.

The Finished Horse

A finished horse is one that's fully trained to run barrels and has proven that he can win. He's also an investment. If you buy a finished horse that doesn't work for you after six months or so and you haven't done anything to devalue him, you should be able to recoup your investment. That's why it's important to be honest about your skills as you set your criteria.

A girl called me looking for a horse that could win at the pro level. She told me she'd rodeoed a lot, but when she showed up it was obvious that she was a novice rider. She hung on to the reins for balance, didn't know anything about leads and was nowhere near ready to ride a horse that could win in amateur rodeo, much less professional rodeo. It's not fair to a finished horse if the buyer isn't capable of riding him correctly. Plus, if the horse is ridden wrong, he can and will quit working.

Buying horses can be a gamble. However, if you buy one that's well-mannered, broke and easy to ride, it'll be easier for you to sell,

TIPS

Checklist for a Finished Horse

A finished horse should fulfill these requirements at a minimum.

- Is a proven winner at the level you want to compete.
- Vet checks sound or if there's a problem, it's manageable.
- Fits you.
- Has no performance problems you can't work around.
- Isn't gate sour.
- Doesn't make wide turns.
- Doesn't run up the fence.
- Doesn't duck off.
- Doesn't crash barrels.

should you need to, and you'll have a better chance of protecting your investment.

Realize at what level the horse is when you buy him. If he wins at open rodeos, don't expect to win at pro rodeos right away. He might get better, but he might also be maxed out in his capabilities.

Time to Adapt

When you buy a finished horse, plan to adapt to him rather than expect him to adapt to you. It's very important – and I can't emphasize this enough – to find out how the former rider has been riding and maintaining the horse. Watch videos to see where the rider's hands are, when she sits down, if she's kicking in between the barrels. See what she does with her body. Check the length of reins. Buy the same bit the horse is used to working in.

Also, don't overlook the things behind the scenes that help make the horse run well, such as exercise routine, practice, feed, supplements and health-care maintenance. Ask the owner everything you can think of. What's her program? Does the horse take a lot of riding? Don't change everything to suit yourself; follow what's been working for your new horse.

If you have the skills needed to make the horse work as the former owner did, you'll likely be able to get with the horse. Just keep working at it. When I bought Magic, his previous owner could make him work right every time. In the beginning, I could get a good run maybe one out of ten. I knew, though, that if his previous owner could be consistent with

him, I could too, and I finally did. Give yourself time to get with your new horse.

There are very few cases where there's not an adjustment period for a new horse-and-rider combination. It takes time to get with a horse, especially if you're a green rider. Give yourself time to get the feel and timing of the way your new horse runs.

Every horse is an individual so plan to take time to adjust to the horse and let him adjust to you. He already has to deal with one big change – that of having a new rider who looks, sounds and feels different. If you change everything else all at once, the horse can get frustrated.

Trial Run

On rare occasions, an owner might let you take the horse home. Only do so if you want to see if he stays sound after a run. Don't run and run and run the horse to see if you can get with him. That's wrong and it takes advantage of the seller. Don't do that to someone else's horse. After you pay the money, you can work to get with him.

Also, don't buy the horse, mess it up because you didn't ride it correctly or maintain its health, then call the previous owner and gripe.

When you try a finished horse, make a practice run. See if the seller will let you try the horse at a barrel race. A lot of horses work well in the practice pen, but then, when you get them to the barrel race, they don't work well no matter who rides them.

If you take the horse to a jackpot or rodeo and he works exactly the same as he does in practice, more than likely you're buying a good horse or it's coincidentally a great fit because that doesn't usually happen.

In the heat of a run, when your and the horse's adrenalin are flowing, is the time when you really find out if you fit your new horse. If the horse feels fine in the practice pen and then scares you in competition, it's not a good fit.

TIPS

Finished Horse Red Flags

Here are some warning signs that tell you something's wrong.

- Owner unwilling to let you make a run on the horse.
- Owner unwilling to let you make a run at a jackpot or rodeo.
- Owner unwilling to let you see the horse the day after you make a run on him.
- Owner placing too much pressure on you to buy the horse.

When I sell one of my horses, I always want the rider to feel comfortable with the horse, so I suggest a practice run to evaluate how well they fit. The buyer might not ride the horse as well as she will in six months, but I can tell if they're going to fit each other.

Your Relationship with the Seller

If you're a serious buyer, have the money and think that, if everything works out, you'd like to buy the horse, make sure that both you and the seller are on the same page with all the sale details clearly understood by both parties. Agree up front what you expect as a qualified buyer and make sure the seller agrees to it. "I want to make one practice run," or "I want to make two practice runs. Then, I want to go to a jackpot." In fairness, don't ask the owner to tolerate more than two runs on her horse. If you want to make a few more runs over several days, that's fine, but clear up these things on the phone before you arrive at the seller's place.

If you decide on a horse but are waiting on money, leave a deposit and clearly agree to the amount of time you need to get your money together. If you can't get it done, typically the seller can keep the money. Write a contract to this effect and both of you sign it.

Agree on how long you have to get the horse vet-checked. If you take the horse off the premises for a pre-purchase exam, there should be well-understood contingencies. Give the seller a check for the animal, and, if he doesn't pass the exam, have an agreement as to how to get him back to the owner and how you get your money back.

Another common contingency includes unforeseen injury to the horse while in your care. For example, if the horse gets hurt in horse trailer and you want to return it to the seller, there should be a liability agreement. Who owns the horse at that point? In most cases, if you take it and break it, it's yours.

The Vet-Check

A vet-check or pre-purchase exam is very important when purchasing a prospect or a finished horse. A prospect can be sound, but have physical conditions or conformational faults that could cause problems later. With a finished horse, you want to have a clear picture of where he is with regard to soundness, so you'll know what you have to do to properly maintain him.

Ask guidance from a veterinarian you have confidence in. Generally, he'll evaluate the horse with flexion tests and by observing the animal moving, then suggest X-rays as needed.

Depending on the purchase price, you might opt for a complete radiology workup as a matter of course. X-rays of the feet, fetlocks, cannon bones, knees and hocks are common. Some horses X-ray clean and are still lame. It's possible the injury hasn't yet made a bone change or is a soft-tissue injury.

I once tried a horse at the owner's house one evening and spent the night at their place in my trailer. The next morning, during breakfast, I noticed the husband wasn't there. I knew the horse had some physical problems, so I asked three different times if he was sound. They told me, "Yes." After breakfast, I excused myself and went to the barn. I saw a bloody spot on the horse's neck that looked like it was from an injection. I got him out of his stall, and he was head-bobbing lame. The moral of the story is "Buyer Beware." Know full well that some people will lie to you to make a sale.

A good horse with some problems is easier to find than a completely sound horse. If you and your vet both feel that you're capable of the level of maintenance needed, you might accept certain problems. Most competition horses have some maintenance issues. Rely on your relationship with your vet and get his opinion on the horse's intended use.

Insurance Policy

There are many reasons to insure your barrel horse. If you can't afford to take the hit on the horse's loss of use from an injury, insure. If you borrowed money from a bank or a friend to buy the horse, you'd better have the animal insured. Or if you're winning barrels races and making money on a horse that's your source of income, you might want to insure for what it would cost to replace him. Also, when you buy a horse, it's very important to have a binder on him from the time you leave the seller's premises.

When I was competing full time and rodeoing for a living, if something happened to my horses, and they were insured, I could take the money and continue on. It's like a truck driver who loses his truck. If you can't replace it, how can you make a living?

Money Can't Buy Gold Buckles

I hear a lot of riders say they want a National Finals Rodeo horse, and I have to caution that the amount of money you pay for a horse is no guarantee you'll get there.

The horse you pay a lot for might have good credentials. He might be a great futurity horse, but when you take him out of the futurity environment he's liable to not be great in rodeos for a few years until he becomes solid.

Just because the horse has been outrunning everyone at the futurities and derbies doesn't mean he's ready for rodeo. I've seen a lot of good futurity and derby horses blown up because their riders tried to make them rodeo horses too quickly.

Know exactly what you're buying and consider what you want to do and where you want to go with a horse. Don't rely on the seller to tell you everything. Rely more on your own judgment to buy a horse. Even an honest owner, with a lot of money at stake, can have a biased opinion.

Although there are now more professionals who train horses and sell them, most people sell their barrel horses because they can't win on them. I've heard every excuse.

"I've got this great horse," says the hopeful seller. "He's awesome, but I need to sell him because I have a family and kids and I can't spend time riding." In reality the horse was actually rearing up and running past barrels. Some excuses or reasons for selling are legitimate and some aren't.

Finally, I think that if you want to be in the horse business, you should never, ever misrepresent your horse to anyone because it'll come back to haunt you. Tell everything you know about your horse to a prospective buyer. In the end, it'll be to your advantage.

The equipment you use can help or hinder your success, and it's essential to know what works and how. Housing your horse is another factor in how your horse feels and how he performs

8

THE TOOLS

If your horse is trained and you're riding correctly, then you can make a run in a different bit or different saddle and still be competitive. But when a hundredth of a second can make a difference, you want the bit that your horse works best in, a saddle that allows you and your horse to perform at the optimum and auxiliary equipment that doesn't interfere, distract or add bulk or weight.

Every horse is different. When it comes to equipment, there's no one perfect formula, so this is an area for experimentation. I'll explain what works for me and what has been good in my experience with different horses, but the choice is up to you.

A Bit About Bits

Find a bit your horse likes – something he's guidable in but not totally controlled. This might sound strange, so I'll explain. In a sport such as reining, riders want to control their horses' every move, but the goal in barrel racing is different. In our sport, because of the tremendous speed involved, a competitor should use something she can guide her horse with. She'd frustrate her horse if she tried to over-control him. Unlike reining horses, barrel horses have to think for themselves.

Bracing on the reins, and therefore the bit, is a common problem for many riders who don't have much of a feel for a horse's mouth. In response, most horses brace against the bit pressure, lunge forward and fight to get free, which interrupts their forward motion. Don't forget – this is a timed event! Add bad hands to a bad mouth and you have a train wreck.

The ideal is to have a soft feel of the horse's mouth with your fingertips. A soft feel lets your horse run free at a speed that's a notch down from a racehorse at top speed. That speed is the pace at which your horse can make a perfect run. You reach this speed not by bracing on the reins, but by riding really smooth.

Of course, we all make mistakes at times with our hands. So, for the most part, depending on your skill level, look for a bit that's a little forgiving of your hands, but always work to make your hands better.

This was the bit Charmayne used on Cruiser to win the world. Scamper's bit was like this but with a slightly higher port.

TIPS

Bit Fit

All horses' mouths are different. Some are shallow or deep, narrow or wide. Some tongues are fat and others thin. How a bit fits and works depends in large part on the conformation of the horse's mouth.

In clinics I see bits on backward or with the curb strap or chain fastened to the wrong part of the bit and even upside-down.

For a bit to work correctly, it has to fit correctly. If you're unsure of whether your horse's bit fits, have someone who really knows check it out for you.

Make sure the headstall fits, too. It shouldn't be so small that it pulls or too big with straps hanging down that could flop and hit the horse's eyes.

Ask yourself, "Did I hold him too much? Would a little less pressure have gotten the job done without losing speed?"

The Snaffle

The snaffle I start young horses in is a shankless bit consisting of two bit rings and a broken mouthpiece. It's good for teaching the horse to give to pressure to the side and to bring his nose around to help get his body in the right position.

Make sure the snaffle you choose is a well-made one that doesn't pinch the corners of the mouth where the rings and the mouthpiece connect.

I start with a smooth mouthpiece. If, after a while, I feel the horse isn't responding to it or is getting really heavy or pulling too much, I put him in a twisted snaffle (but not one of the narrow ones) for a week or two and then go back to the smooth. Make sure your mouthpiece has an arc in it so that it curves over the tongue; otherwise you can pinch the bars of the mouth.

Remember to release when you ride with a snaffle. A horse can get hard-mouthed in a snaffle if you pull on him all the time. Most people tend to be heavier handed in a snaffle. There's also no curb pressure so you rely on just the corner of the mouth on whatever side you'll pulling to stay sensitive. If you ride your horse with a snaffle at progressively faster speeds (that translates to more pull), you can cause callouses, and then the bit won't work.

A properly fitted bit is crucial to the comfort of any horse.

I don't think it's a good idea to make the sides of the mouth sore on a barrel horse. I see some people starting colts, and they get them raw. I can't help but think that this is a bad way to start and a good way to toughen the sides of the mouth.

In my opinion, this type snaffle is a good beginning bit but not one you'll ultimately keep the horse in. Compared to a curb bit, there's very little lift (front-end elevation) in a ring snaffle, and the reaction time (rein response) is slow.

Beginning of Leverage Action

The next step up, for me, is a three-piece jointed mouthpiece bit that slides on very short shanks. The middle joint looks like a dog bone and is attached to the joints on either end making up the three pieces of the mouthpiece. So, instead of breaking in two in the middle, this jointed mouthpiece has three joints, which are comfortable in a horse's mouth. However, you can actually put a curb strap on the bit rings to allow for some slight leverage action, so it's a good transition bit between a regular snaffle and a curb bit. I ride with the reins attached to the snaffle part until the horse is comfortable in it. Then, I move the reins to the shanks and ride with leverage action.

The biggest thing on transitioning from one bit to another is that you get a different feel. It's important to teach young horses that bits are just a way to communicate. I like to ride them in a lot of different bits and build trust – that's real important. Then, when I use a bit for a specific purpose as the horse's style of riding and running develops, he's willing to accept the different bit.

The gag bit, for example, elevates the head some. The gag mouthpiece slides up and down the length of shanks, providing for some leverage action that causes the horse's head to elevate. The way the bit is made determines how much it helps the horse break at the poll. I've tried some gag bits that look right but are constructed so they don't slide up and down smoothly. Some gags really pinch and cut the corners of the mouth and some don't lift (elevate the front end) so you get a dead, "pully" feel. A good gag bit elevates the horse's head and provides good lateral control so you can still get the nose (for lateral flexion). It's a good transition bit when you're coming out of a snaffle.

Some riders use draw gags, where the headstall is connected to the reins through the rings on the bit. When you pull, it pulls on the horse's poll, through the rings, and also pulls the rings up toward the horse's mouth. The gags usually have twisted-wire or narrow mouthpieces, and riders get a lot of response in the beginning. Initially this bit makes horses handle well, but it's fake. The horse is pulled into position, and he can't do much else. When the rider increases speed, the horse is going to get away from the bit eventually.

Shank Bits

The next bit up for me is a three-piece, loose-jawed bit with a little longer shank. My choice is the one made by Mike Quick that has a roller over the center section. It's a bit a lot of horses like. Because of the leverage afforded by the shanks, there's a little more instant lift and not a delayed reaction time in rein pressure. You can still get some nose (lateral bend) with it, as well. Also, because the shanks are hobbled (attached at the bottom by a bar), you get a little indirect rein pressure to keep the horse from being over bent. If a horse is over-bent in the turn, he's generally not as fast as he should be getting around the barrel.

TIPS

Learn from Mistakes

Allow your horse to make mistakes. It's tempting to keep so much control all the time that you never allow the horse to be out of position. You prevent him from ever making a mistake.

At face value, that doesn't sound too bad, but what happens when you turn the horse loose? He'll be unsure of what to do.

It's better to ask the horse to work. Then if he makes a mistake, correct him and ask him again. When you do that, he learns what's correct and what's not. Make it his responsibility because it's going to be his responsibility eventually, anyway, when you start running at top speed. Let him learn how to do things slowly at first, and he'll handle them at speed much better.

I've used the Whisper Bit, which has a hard plastic straight mouthpiece, on horses that either don't like a bit or have gotten afraid of one. This bit really seems to give them confidence. I'm not sure if it's the subtle "give" from the mouthpiece, the non-metal taste and feel or the light weight, but when a horse likes this bit, he really seems to work well in it.

I like to use some hackamores as they seem to work well on barrel horses that don't like bits. I'm not referring to a traditional bosal, but a bitless headgear with a noseband, shanks and a curb (sometimes referred to as a mechanical hackamore). I prefer those with rope nosebands and shorter shanks. The shorter shanks seem to give you a little more nose (lateral control) than others. Likewise, longer-shank hackamores give you lift but less nose.

I'm not a big fan of combination bits – those that combine a mechanical hackamore mechanism with a mouthpiece. These range from the less severe with rope nosebands to the steel noseband variety. Some severe combos catch the side of a horse's mouth and bind it between the curb attachment and the mouthpiece, pinching and cutting the horse. Milder ones seem to cause horses to root into them, over time.

Mule bits are at the very bottom of my list of what you should use. Those pain-producing devices work a time or two, but that's it. You lose any trust and confidence the horse has. You're worse off, eventually. Riders use this type of bit when they cut corners in the training process.

Graduation Time

It's important to stress why I graduate from one bit to another during the training process. It's not about being able to pull more. It's not so the horse can feel the pressure better; it's because he can feel the release faster (the "release" being my release of rein pressure). As my horse advances in training, I give him a more refined tool for communication, where a slight lift speaks volumes.

When you transition from one bit to another, you get a different feel. It's important to teach your horse that bits are a form of communication. I like to ride horses in a lot of different bits and build trust as we go. Then, when I use a bit for a specific purpose as the horse's running style develops, he's willing to accept the different bit.

The bit Scamper ran in was a high-port Sliester. I rode both Scamper and Cruiser in a solid mouthpiece with a port, and they both seemed to like that and work the best in it.

In the beginning, I rode Scamper in a Tom Thumb (a short-shanked bit with a jointed mouthpiece), then went to a grazing bit (a shanked bit with a slight elevation in the mouthpiece port). He was getting away from me in the alleys so Dad put on the high-port Sliester.

Scamper would always run a good pattern in a broken bit. If you look at photos of his early runs in the Tom Thumb, you'd see his turns were very pretty, but they were never as fast as they were in the port bits that kept him more collected.

Cruiser was too "bendy" (had too much lateral bend). I had to ride him two-handed all the way through the pattern for two or three years. As he got older, he was able to graduate into a bit more like Scamper's. His favorite was a low-port Sliester), and he eventually got where he wasn't so bendy.

I use my favorite bits in a refined way to communicate with my horses. My horses like these bits because they've been transitioned to them. They understand them. They're not intimidated by them.

And that's the point. Riders do so much harm jerking on their horses. The horses learn defensive behavior, and the riders lose a valuable avenue of communication. If you jerk, your horse will lose his softness because he's protecting himself.

I see a lot of people bit up their horses and tie their heads around. They do it to the point that they rip and tear the neck muscle tissue. When the horse heals, he actually loses flexion in his neck.

For the most part, horses that don't flex properly (equal to the left and right) were either never taught correctly or they have a dental problem or a neck injury. An equine dentist or a chiropractor can help with the latter two problems.

The number one thing barrel racers do is change bits. They want to find a miracle bit that can fix all their problems. The truth is, a bit isn't going to change anything. If, during a run, you look at the barrels or you're in the wrong position or have bad hands, your horse will still have a problem, no matter which bit you have on him.

Eight Bits:

If I could have just eight bits, they would be the following:

Snaffle – A snaffle bit has two bit rings and a mouthpiece, but no shanks for leverage action. Instead, it puts pressure on the corners of the mouth and is good for bending to the side (lateral flexion).

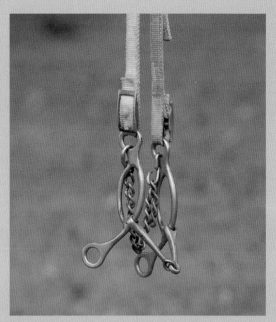

Gag Bit – The mouthpiece of this gag bit slides up and down the bit rings or the length of the shanks, depending on the bit's construction (either snaffle or shank-leverage bit). A pull on the reins causes the mouthpiece to travel upward, thus causing the gag effect. It offers pressure on the corners of the mouth, some tongue pressure and some leverage action.

Three-piece Jointed Mouthpiece – A very mild bit that really conforms to a horse's mouth. Provides pressure on the corners of the mouth, yet transitions nicely with some mild leverage action.

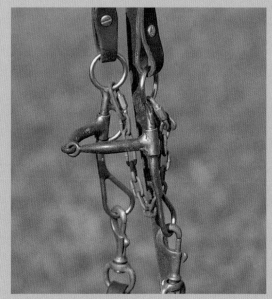

Argentine Snaffle – A good transition bit from the three-piece jointed mouthpiece. Because of the short shank, it offers mild curb action and helps the horse break at poll.

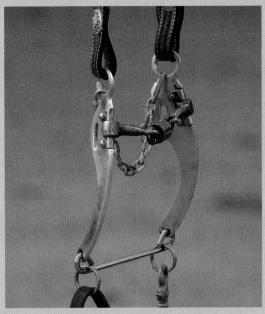

*Jointed Mouthpiece with Roller and Shanks –
This bit has a jointed mouthpiece with a roller
covering the joint. It's loose-jawed and hobbled
(shanks attached at the bottom with a bar).
It provides tongue pressure, as well as
curb action.*

*Rope-Noseband Hackamore with Shanks – The
rope-noseband hackamore with shanks gives
more or less rate depending on the length of
the shank and is more forgiving of bad hands.*

*Whisper Bit – This is a bit with a special hard
plastic mouthpiece. Horses seem to not be
intimidated by it. It comes in a long or short
shank or with D-rings.*

*High-Port Curb – A high-port curb bit offers
palate pressure and curb action with the shanks.*

Tie-Downs and Martingales

Tie-downs are simply a tool to control the horse. However, it'd be better to take the time to properly break the horse in the first place. Then, you wouldn't have to use this gimmick or so-called training device.

Many riders use tie-downs because they say their horses' heads are too high. In reality, the heads are generally in the wrong position because the horses try to protect themselves from bad hands.

What tie-downs do is to steady a rider's hands because the rider can pull the horse's head only so high, then the tie-down stops her. The rider feels the stability from that, but the horse suffers. His head is being pulled one way by the tie-down and another way by the rider's hands. What the tie-down does is trap the horse in a position where he can't protect himself from any pain caused by the bit. Some horses that have worn a tie-down for a long time learn to brace against it, and it becomes a crutch.

If your horse has head-position issues, take the tie-down off and see what your hands are doing. Practice without a tie-down and try to cue without causing your horse to toss his head. Your hands will improve, and your horse will gain confidence and become better broke, as well.

TIPS

Steady Your Hands

Some barrel racers have good hands at slow speeds, but have bad hands at a run. That's often because they can't stabilize their bodies at speed, so they lose control. Other riders do have the physical strength to maintain their position but can't handle the adrenalin rush so their hands get jerky. Here are some tips to help your hands remain steady.

- Slow down your hands by thinking slow, steady movements.
- Work at keeping your seat steady and your hands separated from the movement you absorb with your lower body.
- Do a lot of work at a trot. The horse's head doesn't move at the trot so this is an opportunity to teach your hands to be steady too.
- Move your hands in time with the horse's head movement at a lope to keep the horse at the same pace or to increase his speed. Or you can move your hands in time opposite of the horse's head movement to slow down the horse and collect him.
- Push down with your inside tailbone into the saddle each time the horse's inside hind leg hits the ground in a turn.
- Practice asking softly first, then increasing pressure and releasing just as soon as you get a response.
- Don't balance on the reins. Grab the saddle horn if you need help maintaining your seat.
- Go to some small jackpots and slow down your movements and your speed if adrenalin is your problem. Go often enough to get over it. Make a good run for your horse and yourself and, in time, those emotions will take care of themselves.

Often, riders want to over-control, overwork and overdo with their horse's headgear. Great horses that keep working for a long time are probably ridden in something they like to work in instead of something that forces them to work.

Martingales are another way of forcing a horse into position. It seems as though, much of the time, they put the horse's head into a fixed position, then the horse can't use himself as well.

The best barrel horses I've ever seen have carried their heads in a natural position. There's no need for artificial placement. What happens, though, is that riders see great horses look a certain way around the barrels, then they try to come up with something artificial to make their horses look that way, but it's so unnatural for their horses.

Cavesons (nosebands) are another gimmick. Don't use one to cover up the fact that the horse isn't broke enough, your hands are bad or your horse needs some dental work.

Don't overlook the obvious. Adjust your equipment to make sure everything is on correctly. The right bit on the right horse adjusted the wrong way won't work. Remember, headgear is just part of the equation. If you have the right bit on the horse and are doing everything wrong – dropping you hand, looking at the barrel or the horse is lame or has bad teeth – it's still not going to work.

Spurs

Spurs are tools for the refinement of leg cues, not pain-inducing devices to get horses to run faster. You can get better position (around the barrels) by cuing with spurs correctly.

I can't actually touch my horse's sides because with my height my legs usually hang past the horse's belly. Sometimes cuing with my calf is enough, but, if I need more than leg pressure, I roll my spur up along my horse's side. This is the best way to use spurs. If I need to shape the horse or move him over a little, this works. The key to spurs is having good control of your legs.

I often take spurs off a lot of riders at clinics, especially kids and people with short legs. Because of the length of their legs, both end up jabbing their horses in the ribs when they're balancing or trying to hang on.

Most riders put on spurs to make their horses go faster. You can get a little more reaction out of your horse with spurs, but if you over-use them, you're probably going to make your horse quit running, eventually.

As for type, I like short-shank spurs with really dull rowels that have five flat points. To me, they're the most effective and humane.

Bats, Whips and Over-and-Unders

Whips or bats are encouragement devices used when you need a little extra something or must keep a horse focused on running, instead of looking around. Consider a whip as an extension of your arm to touch the horse where your arm can't reach, but don't use it as a weapon. You're not trying to inflict pain on the horse, just convey a sense of urgency.

If you use a whip, do so in time with your horse's stride. Whip low like a racehorse jockey would, but make sure the whipping produces the desired effect and that you're not actually interfering with your horse.

Don't whip because your horse hits barrels – that only works for a run or two. Go back and fix the problem going slowly. Don't try to run a horse past the problem.

I don't like stinger whips; they tend to hurt and take the run out of horses or really scare them. I like bats with a big leather piece on the end. You can get a horse's attention with that type whip without stinging him badly.

I sometimes carry a whip to tap young or inexperienced horses on the hindquarters to keep forward momentum going around the barrels. You don't have to kick, kick, kick a lazy one. Simply tap to remind him of the need to hurry.

As far as over-and-unders, I like the ones made of heavy leather. They're quick, fast, and don't hang up on your arm.

Pads, Cinches and Breast Collars

I prefer saddle pads made with wool underneath so they don't rub the horse's hair. They're lightweight but still offer protection by absorbing concussion.

Use only the thickness of pads necessary to protect the horse's back without adding bulk. Too many pads can cause you to lose feel of the horse underneath you. Bulky pads force your legs out wide instead of allowing them to hang straight down your horse's sides, and that reduces your ability to use your legs properly. Also, it's hard for a saddle to fit a horse's back correctly when there's too much padding.

Breast collars help stabilize your saddle. When you leave a barrel, the saddle tends to move back. Some horses don't need them, but most do.

I like to use neoprene cinches because they hold the saddle and prevent rolling and sliding. Also, I don't have to cinch up nearly as tight to keep the saddle steady. I don't recommend riding 10 hours a day in one because of the heat it can generate, but if you exercise an hour every day, it's fine. I've found that cinches in 32- or 34-inch lengths are about right for most horses.

As for fit, the cinch rings should end slightly above the horse's elbow. Make sure the cinch is centered so that when you clip the tie-down or breast collar strap to the cinch, the rings won't make the horse sore by rubbing against the inside of his front legs.

I like to ride with a back cinch. I find it steadies the saddle and prevents the back of the saddle from rising when the horse sets up before turning a barrel. Don't tighten the back cinch like you would on a rope horse. Adjust it so it lies flat against the horse's belly. Some horses don't like back cinches but that's rare. Make sure it's hobbled to the front cinch. If you don't, it could act as a flank strap, and you'll end up in a rodeo.

Saddle Savvy

One of the biggest problems I see with many saddles is that they can put you in the wrong position. Some have stirrups set so far back that your legs fall behind you, which makes you fall forward as the horse accelerates or turns.

Correctly hung stirrups allow your legs to fall naturally at your sides. You should be able to stand straight up in the stirrups in one easy motion. You can stay balanced in such a saddle, making it a lot easier to stay in stride with your horse.

Another problem is that some saddles are constructed with large swells to hold you in tightly. Many riders use them as a crutch. Also, like stirrups hung too far back, they don't allow you to move with the horse, so you can't stay in sync with him.

I'm also not that fond of treeless saddles because I don't think you can get out of them that well. They sit you down on the horse so it's hard to move in them.

When it comes to saddling, first make sure your horse's back is clean of any dirt, sand or grit that can irritate the skin. Taking the time to brush properly will help prevent back soreness and also make your horse's coat healthy.

As far as saddle position, don't set your saddle too far forward on your horse's back.

You should be able to get a hand in between the cinch and the horse's elbow. A too-forward saddle places excessive pressure on a horse's shoulders, interfering with their movement.

Always remember to lift the front of the pad slightly just before you set the saddle down on the horse's back. As the saddle slips into place it allows the hair on the horse's withers to be smooth, too.

Once the saddle is in place, take your left hand and lift from underneath the front of the pad. That will give you a little more room than you need, and, when you slide the saddle back down, it won't pull tightly over the withers. That, in turn, will help prevent the withers from becoming sore if the pad presses down on them.

Sometimes even a well-fitted saddle can make a horse sore if the rider is getting on the horse incorrectly. You can make a horse sore from getting on, especially if you're overweight. To mount correctly, think of taking a big step straight up, instead of hanging and pulling yourself so that the saddle shifts and bruises the horse's back.

Finally, check regularly to see if your saddle tree is broken. Set the saddle on concrete, resting on its horn. Push directly down on the back of the saddle and look at where the seat meets the swell in the front of the saddle. If you can see any movement at all there, have the saddle checked right away. A broken tree can make a horse stop working.

I helped design two saddles, the "Charmayne Record Breaker" and the extra-light weight "Scamper." They seem to fit most horses, and the stirrups are hung in the correct position to help you maintain your seat throughout the run.

Protective Boots

Protective leg boots are very important. Failing to have on overreach boots can put you out of competition for a month if your horse steps on his front feet with his hind feet during a run. Also, horses that really like to get down low in the turns need heel protection. Burning skin and hair will make a horse quit working to the point that he won't drop his hindquarters into the ground at all.

Use overreach boots, plus leg boots front and back because you can't control the ground. If you hit deep ground or a slippery spot, your horse can hit himself.

I prefer lightweight boots that conform comfortably to a horse's leg and are easy to put on correctly.

Stirrups

Aluminum stirrups with rubber grips as treads on the bottom are my favorite because they help hold feet in the stirrups much better than rawhide or wood stirrups.

Stirrup-length adjustment is important because you want your stirrups to be the correct length for your body. One easy way to measure for proper length is to sit in the saddle, take your feet out of the stirrups and watch where the bottom of the stirrups hits. It should be at your ankle bone or a tad higher, whatever length makes you feel confident during a run. You should be able to bend at your knees slightly as you sit in the saddle. From that position, you have ability to keep your feet in the stirrups and to use your legs for cuing.

If the stirrups are too short, you won't be able to move like you should or sit down deep in the saddle in the turns. If they're too long, you might get thrown back in the saddle and out of rhythm with your horse as he starts his run or leaves a barrel. You could also lose a stirrup.

Note: Riding boots can have thick or wide soles, so, for safety's sake, make sure you can

A high-quality pad provides adequate room above the horse's withers.

A properly fitted saddle should sit down on a horse's back and stay secure during acceleration and in the turns. Note that the pad affords plenty of protection, but isn't overly thick.

107

Even on great ground, a horse can take a misstep. Having leg boots on is your insurance against your horse hitting himself.

get your feet out of the stirrups. Either buy different boots or bigger stirrups, but give yourself a way to exit the saddle should you need to. Stuffing big boots into small stirrups isn't wise. You could get hung up and possibly dragged. Also, if you change boots, adjust your stirrup length to take into account the thicker or thinner soles.

Optional Equipment

Because everyone knocks down barrels at some point, many riders wear shin guards to protect themselves. It's completely your choice as to whether or not you want to wear them. It's probably a good idea to put them on to prevent injury or re-injury if they give you more confidence or make you ride bolder. Personally, I don't use them because if I hit a barrel I feel it was probably my fault and I could've done something to prevent that from happening.

Overall, as far as equipment goes, put on your horse just what he needs and is comfortable working in. Equipment should fit, be streamlined and proportionate to your horse. Don't put on extra things because they look cool. You're there to run barrels. Ultimately the thing that looks the most cool is having a horse that works well and wins.

Stabling

Your horse should have adequate shelter from the environment. Anything you can provide to make him more comfortable will only help him be less stressed and less fatigued.

In your corral, remove any rocks your horse could step on and get sore. Also, make sure

TIPS

Braids

Braiding long manes is beneficial in barrel racing. Braids keep the mane hair from becoming tangled in your hands as you turn the barrels.

TIPS

Ground Rules

The ground can make or break the run and learning about ground is important for success as a barrel racer. Often, barrel racers are quick to criticize any variation in ground at an event, but never notice the truly awful surface they work their horses on every single day at home.

If your home ground is hard, concussion will put extra wear and tear on your horse. Make sure your ground provides good traction and is deep enough to absorb some of the shock.

Be able to water and work your ground regularly. Not only will the quality of your workouts improve, but your horse will also stay more sound.

your corral is made of sturdy material, such as wood or metal, not wire. Wire fences work fine in a pasture, but not in a small corral. If another horse is close by, they might fight or play too hard and someone will get hurt.

Probably one of the worst things you can do is keep your horse in an area that holds water, forcing him to stand in water or mud. Your horse won't have a clean, dry place to lie down and rest. It's also horrible on the horse's feet and can cause thrush.

If you stall your horse, how you maintain the stall is important for your horse's health and comfort. The stall should have soft ground or thick rubber mats under the bedding. That's more comfortable for the horse that has to stand for hours on end, plus he won't skin his hocks when he lies down.

Use a fan over the stall for cooling and ventilation purposes. Also, clean all urine spots, as well as the manure. Manure is where flies breed and lay eggs. If you clean your stall every day, it doesn't turn into a huge project.

Be sure to get a stalled horse out each day both for work and for play. Horses are made to roam and forage, and it's not healthy for them to live in a 12- by 12-foot prison.

Turn your horse out to relax in a safe area each day.

You've got a wonderful partner that takes you to the winner's circle or will one day. Your job is to keep that partner feeling his best, and diet plays a huge part of that. A well-nourished horse has a strong immune system and can better withstand the rigors of training and the stress of the road.

9

NUTRITION FOR FITNESS

When it comes to nutrition, maintaining your barrel horse takes some education on your part to discover what's best. Think of your horse as a finely-tuned racing machine. Since you ask him to give you top performance, you, in turn, must give him the best fuel you can.

Common Sense Feeding Formula

There's no one feeding formula that works for all horses because each horse is different with varying nutritional needs. You have to tailor the program to fit the individual. Through the years, though, I've been able to come up with a program that I think works for most horses. However, it's still a matter of looking at your horse and evaluating his condition.

The best way, in my opinion, is to feed four times a day and keep good quality hay in front of your horse at all times. From the first year I hit the road with Scamper, I fed him four times a day. I've had barrel racers ask me why in the world I feed multiple times, which, by the way, is the approach most racehorse trainers take with racehorses. The reason is that, early in my career, I was lucky to work with a nutritionist, Dr. Gordon Wooden, who also happened to be a good family friend. Dr. Wooden explained to me how the equine digestive system works. Horses are foraging animals by nature and that means they're designed to eat constantly. In the wild, horses graze most of the day; their stomachs are seldom empty. Horses in captivity, however, are often fed at infrequent intervals or fed once or twice per day. There are times in their day when there's little if any feed in their stomachs. This isn't an ideal situation and can cause myriad problems.

Horses don't salivate without chewing, so an empty stomach and lack of buffering from saliva combined with stress make ulcers a major problem for all horses, but especially performance horses.

Ideally, it's best to always have hay in front of your horse. Having constant access to hay increases chewing time and salivation thus helping buffer the acid being continuously produced in the horse's stomach. Even small bites of hay increase salivation and its buffering capacity.

A good roughage diet consists of grass hay along with some alfalfa. Be careful with feeding too much alfalfa, though. Some horses can't tolerate it because of its high protein and energy content. Horses that are fed a lot of alfalfa have to be exercised frequently.

To prevent the possibility of blister beetles in alfalfa, I try to get hay out of states that don't have the beetle problem. I feel more comfortable getting the hay out of New Mexico or Colorado.

Feed is Fuel

If you want your horse to be an athlete, you've got to give him the fuel he needs to perform. The right fuel can make him feel good, have energy and be mentally fit. The wrong feed can make him too high or too lethargic.

The amount of feed is important. It's wrong to think that if you don't feed a nervous horse as much, he'll get better. Often that type horse gets shaky and nervous because he needs feed.

Some riders even try to correct a performance problem by starving the horse, and sometimes they get them so weak and tired that this works. However, it's a temporary fix and when they go back to feeding the horse, the problem is still there. Horses need sufficient energy to be able to learn and perform.

With a more nervous-type horse, the more weight you can keep on him, the better he's going to be. Make sure to leave hay in front of him all the time because he'll feel a lot better with a full stomach and won't be quite as nervous.

For a laid-back horse, with a slower metabolism, feed small amounts at least three times a day, but better four.

As a rule of thumb, feed more during peak travel times, as your horse needs more for energy and calories because of the increased exercise. You'll also need to feed more in extreme weather conditions.

On the road, it's a challenge to feed correctly and consistently. There are a lot of feed companies but even the same brand can differ from mill to mill. The content might be the same, but the balance might be different. Changing feeds abruptly can disrupt a horse's gastro-intestinal system, inviting colic. So it's best not to change feeds if at all possible. When I was rodeoing, to prevent having to switch feeds I loaded 40 bags of feed on a pod on top of the trailer. That way, my horses got the same quality feed no matter where we were in the country.

Breakfast of Champions

Scamper, Cruiser and all my horses eat a ration of roasted grains. My father worked closely with Dr. Wooden on cattle and horse rations and this led to me using roasted grains as the main staple of my horses' grain diet. Roasted milo works well for horses because they assimilate it easily. Reducing the amount of gastric acid needed to break down the food can help eliminate the occurrence of body soreness and stomach ulcers, which I'll explain more in detail later.

In 2004, I formed a partnership with Gore Brothers Feed Company in Comanche, Texas, to make this roasted feed for the public, and we named it Scampers Choice. This feed will initially be available at feed stores in Texas, Oklahoma, New Mexico and Louisiana and there are plans to expand the distribution.

My goal was to create a feed that supplied all the horses' nutritional needs in correctly balanced proportions. Scamper's Choice is constructed to be metabolically balanced, and I can tell with my own horses that they're focused and calm but still able to stop the clock.

A Good Kind of Fat

Scamper's Choice also has some added fat for extra energy. Adding fat to the diet benefits the equine athlete in several ways. First, the volume of grain can be reduced because of the increased energy density of the feed. This is also a much safer way to feed because less grain decreases gastric upsets and the chance of grain-overload founder.

Secondly, feeding high-fat diets help adapt the horse to using body fat as an energy source. There's much more energy stored in the body as fat than any other energy source. This is advantageous during warm-up and certain types of exercise, specifically aerobic.

Unlike carbohydrates, fat minimizes any negative impact the energy source can have on the horse's attitude. Fat doesn't make a horse high, but it does make him consistently feel good. Fats can have a positive impact on everything from inflammation to reproduction.

Also, high-fat diets are a cooler way to feed. They don't generate internal heat (caused by digestion) like fiber (carbohydrates) and protein can. Lastly, a high-fat diet can also decrease tying up or body soreness, which is often the result of feeding high levels of carbohydrates.

Ulcers, the Hidden Threat

When I was running Cruiser, I cut back the grain in his ration and increased the fat. That helped his stress level and body soreness because he didn't secrete as much gastric acid, which also decreased the chance for ulcers.

You might not be aware that horses can suffer internally. Horses with ulcers generally

TIPS

Group Feed

If you feed several horses in one pen together, see if there's a timid one that's not getting enough. Another might be getting the same amount but actually need more. In either case, you'll need to feed them separately.

Measure your feed and be consistent with your feeding times and amounts.

The texture of the roasted milo is extremely palatable and easily assimilated by horses.

look gutted up, are sunken at the flanks and have a dull haircoat. They tend to become more excitable the closer to the event, and they might even show behavior problems, such as not wanting to enter the arena. They also fall apart in competition because they can't deal with the pain. You must treat ulcers to heal them. Consult your veterinarian for treatment options.

Also, adapting their feeding program can have a huge effect in how they feel and in how they perform.

Picky about Protein

Don't mistake a feed's crude protein content with energy. In fact, having to use protein as an energy source is a drain on your horse's energy. The contradiction is that it requires energy to break down the protein so it can be used for energy. Therefore, using protein as an energy source is both an inefficient and costly way to provide energy.

Exercise doesn't alter the percent of protein required in the horse's diet. For example, a horse that receives two pounds of a 10-percent protein feed when he's lightly ridden receives .2 pounds of protein from that feed. If you ride him more, you'll need to increase his grain to meet the increased energy demands.

Cruiser (top), at age 13, and Scamper, at 28, have had the benefit of a good diet all their lives, and they both look great for their age. Good flesh coverage, shiny hair, alert expression and energy are all indications of a good nutrition program.

But if you increase his grain intake to three pounds, then he would receive .3 pounds of protein. My roasted milo ration increases protein intake by 50 percent, so you don't have to feed a lot to provide adequate protein.

Vitamins

Any good feed should have a wide array of vitamins, which are necessary for a horse's overall health. Of the two classes of vitamins, fat-soluble and water-soluble, over-supplementation of certain fat-soluble vitamins is a possibility. Vitamins A and D are both fat-soluble vitamins and are stored in the horse's body. Horses exposed to pasture or even newly baled hay can store enough vitamin A in the liver for six months. An upper safe limit for vitamin A content is about 8,000 IU per pound of dry feed.

Other Feeding Challenges

Along with good feed, pay attention to your horse's dental needs. If your horse has bad teeth, he's not going to get the most nutritional value from whatever you feed him. If he's sound, healthy and happy, he'll thrive on good feed. If he's not, then no matter how good your nutrition program is, he won't be or look his best.

Nutrition also has an effect on hair and on the horse's hoofs. Even with a great farrier working from the outside, you might have to address the inside. Some horses are fine on a good feeding program, but others have genetically bad feet, which require special hoof supplements.

Electrolytes are another area of concern for barrel racers. They help a horse recover from fluid-loss due to over-exertion. Add an electrolyte supplement on the days your horse sweats heavily. Electrolytes come in various forms – paste, powders, pellets and liquid. Tip: If a horse isn't drinking well, try adding sea salt to his feed to encourage thirst.

I'm a fan of using as many natural remedies as possible. For example, lysine is really good to combat viruses – and there are other supplements, such as vitamin C for combating viruses and helping stressful situations. Arnica and trameel can be used topically or orally, and they're good for trauma or bruising. Echinecea helps support the immune system, plus if a horse has had pneumonia or any type fluid in the lungs, it could help him recover faster.

If your horse does have to go through a round of antibiotics, feed him probiotics to replace the good bacteria.

The Immune System and Stress

Feeding correctly also helps boost the horse's immune system. Stress might have the greatest negative impact on the horse's overall health. It causes the immune system to weaken, alters the endocrine function and might also play a role in the horse's excitability.

Because you have to travel to compete, you have to keep your horse in different stalls. You never know if the horse that was in the stall before was sick. If your horse's immune system is running at a high level and he comes into contact with germs, his body can fight them. But if his immune system is impaired, the horse is at risk for catching a disease.

Horses are often given steroids to help alleviate a breathing problem or body soreness, to increase their appetite and enhance their performance. But steroids suppress the immune system, and, if overused, they can cause a horse to founder or at the very least burn out.

Just Say "No!"

Unfortunately, many riders give their horses drugs to try to get more speed out of them. That's never been part of my program. Scamper lasted 10 years because I never abused him with drugs. I took exceptionally good care of him. He always had the nutrients, vitamins, minerals and supplements he needed, plus the best dental and veterinary care. Also, he was fortunate not to have been treated with an antibiotic for every little thing, and, if he was tired and needed a break, he got one.

The War on Worms and Bugs

It's absolutely imperative to deworm your horse regularly. Worms rob a horse of vitality and the nutrients you feed him. Large concentration of horses require deworming more often as do horses in warmer climates where the winter cold is less likely to kill parasite eggs.

I prefer not to deworm by using a stomach tube because it can cause damage. I prefer the paste dewormers, and the feed-through dewormers seem to work well, too. Check with your veterinarian for what's the best for your area and situation.

The same thing goes for vaccinations. Do the research and know what's best for you, your horse and your area. If you travel out of state, you'll need annual or semi-annual Coggins tests for equine infectious anemia before you can safely cross state lines.

TIPS

What Is Noni Juice?

According to Dr. Richard Godbee, nutritionist for Tahitian Noni Equine Essentials, Morinda citrifolia or noni is an herb from the South Pacific region that has been used for over 2,000 years as a natural remedy for many problems in humans.

M. citrifolia is an adaptogenic compound. This group of plants was initially studied in the 1950s and '60s by Soviet exercise physiologists as a nutritional supplement for their elite athletes. Work done on humans and horses indicates adaptogenic properties include enhanced uptake of glucose by the cell, improved gaseous exchange in the lungs and improved oxygen utilization. They also help the body (cells) adapt to adverse conditions, such as stress.

There's some indication that adaptogens might also improve lipolysis or the breakdown of fat as an energy source. All of these are very important to the equine athlete. Adaptogens are also immune-system modulators. Specific additives in some brands include flaxseed oil for its high level of omega-3 fatty acid, sunflower oil for its level of omega-6 fatty acid, soy lecithin as a source of phospholipids and vitamin E.

The omega-3 fatty acids have an anti-inflammatory effect. Vitamin E is both an antioxidant and immune-system modulator. Soy lecithin is important in brain development and peripheral nervous system function. This might play a role in horses' ability to focus, thus impacting horses' attitudes.

Help for Joints

It's a good idea to keep your horse on some sort of joint-maintenance program. Depending on the horse, that might be glucosamine, chondroitin and/or hyaluronic acid – either fed orally or injected. Your goal is to help your horse feel his best and last as long as he can.

Even if a horse doesn't have joint problems, he might take a bad step running somewhere. If you have him on joint supplements, as well as provide him with proper nutrition, the resulting injury might not be as prolonged or serious as it would've been.

A little ache that your horse might show no sign of can still affect the clock in a barrel race. That's how most injuries start out – so small you can't see them. If you continue using the horse and he can't heal properly, it can turn into something worse.

Injectable joint medications, such as Legend® (hyaluronic acid) and Adequan® (polysulfated glycosaminoglycan), must be prescribed by a veterinarian. If a horse has some problems with soreness after he works, try them to see if you notice any improvement, but realize that not all horses respond to them.

Your veterinarian might recommend an anti-inflammatory, but be aware that they can have negative side effects. Some types, such as phenylbutazone (a.k.a. "bute") and flunixin meglumine (Banamine®), might be hard on the stomach, liver and kidneys and can cause ulcers if over-used. Some anti-inflammatories are better for swelling and joints, while others seem to work best on muscles, tendons and ligaments.

Miracle Juice

I believe that using noni juice was a huge factor in winning my last world title with Cruiser. Noni juice works on a cellular level to keep cells healthy; its antioxidants get rid of free radicals that work on the body's healthy cells.

With the noni juice, Cruiser handled the stress, focused better and didn't get nervous. Plus, he stopped the clock faster.

I believe that adding noni juice to your feeding program can improve your horse's health and alleviate having to use steroids or other chemicals that are detrimental to a horse. If you do have to give an anti-inflammatory, noni juice makes it work better, and sometimes feeding noni is enough without having to give any pain-relieving drug.

I gave Cruiser two ounces orally morning and evening. I like to give it on empty stomach with a large syringe. On days I competed I gave it six to eight hours before I was up.

Noni juice actually works as well on horses as it does on people. When any of my horses get little bellyaches or snotty noses from weather changes, I give them some noni juice for three or four days instead of an antibiotic. I also use it on minor cuts and scrapes.

All the horses I compete with are on it. When I first found out about it, it seemed too good to be true. You might not see results immediately, but give it three to four weeks to build the horse's health from the inside out.

Note: Noni juice can be purchased online, from brand-name distributors or at human health-food stores. Check online for noni juice specifically targeted for horses.

Arm yourself with as much knowledge about nutrition and equine health care as you can. Talk to an expert in your area. Often, you can find one through your county agricultural extension office, or if you live near a university with an equine program, you might check their faculty for experts in various health-care fields.

*Once you've gotten your
horse on a good nutrition
program, he needs proper exercise
to complete the fitness equation.
Only with the right diet and exercise
combination will you have the
athlete that's healthy and fit
enough to be a
consistent winner.*

10

EXERCISE
AND
CONDITIONING

Fit horses are strong, prepared athletes that aren't as prone to injury in competition as their unfit counterparts. Getting your horse into shape and keeping him in shape take time. Over the years I've watched some successful riders who didn't give their horses the time they needed. Guess what? They went through a lot of horses.

Plan to spend an hour and a half with your horse each day, as a minimum. If you rush out and throw a saddle on your horse, then lope around the arena for five minutes, work through the barrels and put him up, you're not spending the right amount of or kind of time. Not only does that scenario work against his fitness, but it's also nerve-wracking for him.

119

A ride in the pasture is relaxing for most horses.

Long-trotting helps lengthen the stride, stretches the legs and increases flexibility, while building strength.

Warm-up Routine

Some horses have a lot of energy and their minds go in a hundred different directions. I like to ride my horses outside of the arena. My daily routine is to walk and trot in the pasture for about 20 to 30 minutes no matter what horse I'm on. It's so good for the horse's mind. You're so much further ahead that way than if you just take your horse from the barn straight to the arena.

From the pasture, I walk the horse into the arena and warm him up by long-trotting in both directions, which stretches his muscles and lengthens his stride. I then lope some circles, stop and back a step. During this process, I ask him to give his head both ways. All these things are important because they reinforce the basics. They also help the horse get tuned-in to me even before we work.

Finally, this type warm-up provides an "instrument check" for the rider. For example, if a horse doesn't want to bend to one side and he has been willing to do so in the past, I know that something is likely causing discomfort. It might be a sore neck or a tooth or just that he's stressed and resisting. Either way, I know something needs attention.

The goal of the warm-up is to get the horse loosened up, but not ridden down. Later, the warm-up's repetition and familiarity will calm and reassure him at the barrel race.

A Sensible Workout Program

Exercise is important – ride your horse regularly. Long-trot everyday. Use your horse's physical condition to determine how much trotting you do. Then lope both ways of the arena – again the amount of time is dependent on the horse's condition. Lope large and small circles. Lope until the horse relaxes and tunes into you. You want him to lope on a loose rein and not look around at other distractions.

Work on his flexibility by bending him side-to-side, flexing at the poll and backing. That will help him warm up, become flexible and in the right frame of mind to do slow work around the barrels. In this mindset, he can learn.

Separate the long-trotting and loping with walking in between to let your horse catch his breath. Also, occasionally stop and let your horse stand quietly and relax. Stand in front of the barrel pattern, showing him that it can be a safe zone. For many horses this is a very

TIPS

Sample Week Working Schedule

Saturday – barrel race

Sunday – day off

Monday – light workout, with some walking, then long-trotting in the pasture. Spend some time in the arena, but cut the normal loping time in half.

Tuesday – full workout. Pasture ride first, then spend 10 to 15 minutes walking and checking the basics before you work the barrels.

Wednesday – repeat Tuesday's full workout.

Thursday – repeat the previous two days, but if you haven't made a run the week before, make a run or breeze your horse.

Friday – light workout (See Monday.).

Saturday – barrel race again.

stressful spot; they paw, showing insecurity and letting you know they want to get out of there. Standing quietly by a barrel helps them relax.

Remember to cool down the horse by walking him until he's cool and starting to dry.

You might have to adjust your exercise program for a horse that has physical challenges, such as hock and feet problems. With this type horse, you might stop him only once or twice in your workout. Any more might aggravate the condition, but some exercise is crucial for blood flow and circulation to keep him from getting stiff as it promotes healing.

On a horse with no problems, trot and lope around the barrels. Don't make all-out runs, but work to keep him flexible for the bending and turning you do in a run. Lope circles both ways, stop and roll back on the fence a couple of times to keep your horse in shape for the physical demands of barrel runs.

A barrel horse doesn't have to run around barrels everyday to keep in running shape. Long-trotting and loping get the heart rate up and maintain fitness during the week if you're going to a competition each weekend or so.

If you're not going to barrel races for a while, occasionally breeze your horse in the pasture for a hundred yards or so to open up his lungs. Alternatively, you might make a run at home if your ground is in good condition.

Loping circles builds wind and strength.

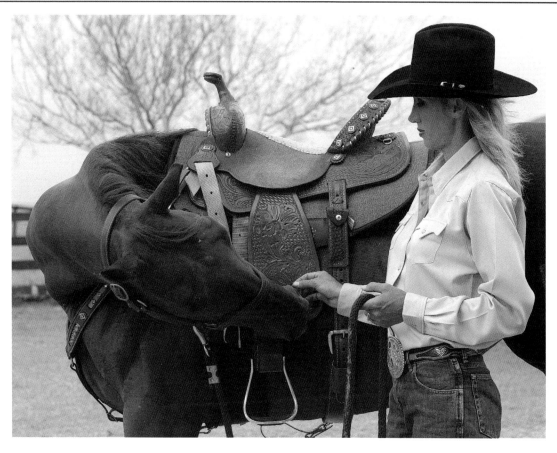

Charmayne encourages her horse to really flex his neck to get the treat.

When you do make a run, whether at home or on the road, evaluate your horse's condition. How hard does he breathe? How fast does he recover? He should be back to normal in about 10 minutes. If not and if there are no extenuating circumstances (extreme heat or physical problems), then he needs to be in better shape.

I recommend working your horse five days a week. Horses are like people in that they do well with a day off. If for example, you compete on Saturday night and aren't going anywhere until the following weekend, take Sunday off, then give light exercise on Monday and the next day get back to your daily work. (See "Sample Week Working Schedule.")

Stretching Strategies

Doing some laps around the arena at a long-trot or extended trot really stretches the hamstrings. You can simulate the stretching the horse will do in the run by spending some time long-trotting, and at the same time asking him softly to flex first one side, then the other.

Another good way to get your horse to stretch his neck muscles is to make him really reach for treats. You can do so from on the ground or horseback, but I prefer the latter.

While in the saddle, ask the horse to bend with the reins to each side, or put a treat in your hand and offer it to your horse. Make him bring his nose all the way to your foot, to stretch the neck and shoulder muscles and keep them loose and supple. This also helps prevent soreness.

There are lots of stretches to help your horse remain supple and flexible. *Equine Acupressure: A Working Manual* (Tallgrass Publishers LLC) by Nancy Zidonis, Amy Snow and Marie Soderberg is one good book with great examples.

Telltale Hair

Daily grooming before and after riding is all part of conditioning. It makes your horse feel good and keeps the oil distributed in his coat. Plus, as you cover every inch of his body, you might discover soreness or swelling.

You might need to use blankets and sheets on your horse for his comfort in inclement weather. However, barrel horses don't have to be show-slick because their event isn't judged, but it's still a good idea to not have extremely long hair. That way he won't get too hot indoors in the winter. When your horse has long hair, it takes a lot of energy for the horse to cool down.

With short hair, he'll dry and cool down faster. But remember, unless you're willing to really go the extra mile to keep him warm, you don't want him completely slick in the winter.

I believe the ideal haircoat is somewhere between short and long, where the horse has some protection from the cold yet isn't hairy and hot.

Obviously, you can tell by looking at a horse if his haircoat is shiny or dead-looking. Horse hair should be shiny and slick no matter what the length. If it's not, then you have a problem that's probably based on nutritional deficiencies.

Don't confuse dull hair with sun-bleached hair, though. For instance, I have a horse that doesn't perform well if I keep him in a stall, even if I ride him every day. However, if I keep him in the pasture, he works great. He's dark brown and the sun bleaches him so much he looks buckskin. But I live with that because I know he likes to be out with other horses and that's what relaxes him. Most horses, especially young ones, ride better when they're able to be outside.

I like all my horses to get out some time each day just for recreation. Older horses especially need to get out. It's better for their circulation.

Also, the larger the stall, the better for the horse. Runs connected to stalls allow even more exercise.

Care and Conditioning on the Road

It's important to take care of your horse's needs as you haul down the road for competition. For example, before you load your horse onto a trailer, take the time to walk him around. This lets him stretch out his muscles and get his circulation going before the long trip.

Then, on the road, unload your horse and walk him every five hours or so. When you get to the event, make sure you walk him around before putting him into a stall or tying him.

In the morning before you feed, get him out of the stall and walk him. If you can, put him in a corral so he can move out a lot more. Horses were just not meant to be penned up in small areas.

How and where you keep the horse while on the road affects his condition, as well. For example, a horse with sore front feet will have a harder time being stabled on the concrete floors found at some fairgrounds around the country. Even extra shavings in the stall might not help him. He probably needs to be kept where he can move around and not have to stand on a hard surface.

If you know your horse requires special attention, call ahead and find where you can stay and turn your horse out if that's something he needs. Also, with a horse that gets sore and needs extra padding, bring rubber mats to put down in his stall.

When you're a barrel racer, your most important job is to take care of your horse and yourself. Spend time hand-walking your horse so he's not just left in the stall. Find some grass for him to eat. If you have a horse that has problems – sore feet, knees, hocks – don't stable him on concrete or even on hard ground for any length of time.

Final Thoughts

As you get to know your horse, you'll find the perfect workout for him. Some horses require more walking after their workout or between segments of the work.

Any time you work your horse, watch for signs of exhaustion. A tired horse is more easily injured from strain or fatigue causing a misstep or just not having enough strength left to support himself.

Finally, remember that the horse's mental attitude is influenced by the contact you have with the horse everyday. It shouldn't just be drill after drill, day after day. Go for a trail ride and let him play in the creek as you cross it. Chase some steers out of the pen at a team roping. Give him a chance to enjoy other aspects of life.

TIPS

In the Swim

If your horse is coming back from an injury, swimming is a great way to get him into shape, plus it offers him non-weight-bearing exercise. Beware, though, that swimming doesn't actually get him into running shape.

I can ride 20 head of horses in a day and be fine, but I can go skiing and be sore. The point is, I used a different set of muscles for skiing than for riding.

It's the same for horses. Swimming gets them back into condition, but it won't get them into shape to run barrels.

Letting the horse relax might be as simple as taking the time to let him roll. This world champion (Cruiser) sure enjoys it.

To maintain a horse in optimum health and condition, it takes a team. Since every hundredth of a second counts, you need to make sure that your team represents the best in knowledge, skill and dedication. Veterinarians, chiropractors, farriers, dentists and acupuncturists can all play a part in your success if you assemble a team of the best professionals.

11

YOUR PARTNERS IN SOUNDNESS

It takes a team to win in barrel racing, and it's your responsibility to assemble the best team you can. Find knowledgeable professionals with whom you feel comfortable, but don't expect to turn all health issues over to them. Ultimately, the decisions are yours. Listen to the health-care professionals' advice, then make informed decisions for your horse's welfare.

Be aware of how important this aspect of your barrel racing is. So many times at my clinics, I see riders who've spent the money for the clinic and are ready to buy a new bit or piece of equipment that'll help them win more, but they're not willing to address the horse's health and soundness issues, which should be their first concern.

The Veterinarian

One of the most important team members is your veterinarian. Your vet will know what's normal for your horse and how his injuries will affect his performance.

Dr. Robert Lewis in Elgin, Texas, has taken care of my horses since 1991 when he did surgery on Scamper's knee. I've remained his client ever since and continue to respect his knowledge on how to keep a horse sound.

Scamper and I won the Houston Livestock Show in 1991, then the next day Dr. Lewis performed the surgery. After the surgery, I did anything and everything Dr. Lewis told me might help, and I was diligent about it. The first two weeks, I kept Scamper quiet. After two weeks, I applied cold therapy by putting him in turbolator boots three times a day. After that I started with a sweat at night, alternating heat and cold and eventually I added laser therapy. As I went along, I hand-walked Scamper every day for increasing lengths of time. I also manually flexed the knee each day. I followed Dr. Lewis' recuperation directions to the letter, and sooner than expected Scamper was back to normal.

When it comes to veterinary care, don't expect a vet to give you good guidance if you don't tell him the complete story or follow the treatment protocol exactly. You can increase the likelihood of your horse coming back after an injury by working hard at rehabilitation. Performing a horse's rehab only halfway results in slower or incomplete recovery. Take the time to give your horse every advantage.

Barrel racing is strenuous. With the kind of pressure a horse's hock undergoes in a turn, it's easy to see why keeping a horse sound is a full-time job.

Barrel horses take a lot of concussion on their joints, especially in the hocks and stifles. With joint problems, relieving the pain almost always results in better performance. Neglecting to treat the inflammation invites secondary osteoarthritis so there's definitely a down-side to not treating joint problems.

According to Dr. Lewis, many of his barrel-racing clients come to him because they feel their horses aren't as sharp as they were or not as fast.

"Barrel horses back off on the run or turn in a time that's not as fast or they fret and don't want to go into the arena," says Dr. Lewis, referring to potential soundness problems. "Much of the time, it's not an obvious limp. Lameness and soreness in hind limbs especially are hard to pick out."

Every horse has a pain tolerance. Some horses, though, continue to work, even though they're in pain. Be on the lookout for any signs of soreness. Joint problems could be surfacing without you knowing it.

Using anti-inflammatories is an option for horses that are intermittently sore, but side effects are possible with continual use and can include gastrointestinal problems.

Other options are hyaluronic acid injections, and your veterinarian might opt to use them in combination with other corticosteroid products.

Joint injections can be expensive, and Lewis warns that there's a risk of infection any time you invade the joint with a needle. Also, individual horses might be hypersensitive to the injections, and the process is painful. Horses are usually sedated.

Time off after hyaluronic injection is normally 48 hours.

Beware of overdoing cortisone-type medications. They're suspected of having detrimental effects on cartilage with chronic overuse and in large doses.

Barrel racers often hear that a hock soundness problem becomes better after the affected joint fuses. Generally, that situation refers to the three tarsal joints (which make up the hock) between the tibia and cannon bone. These joints sit on top of each other and are shock absorbers with no range of motion. With enough damage the joints lose cartilage, and, when they do, the joint fuses. In an X-ray, you can't see the individual joints any more.

The truth is some horses do well with fused joints, according to Dr. Lewis. "I've seen some horses so sore that nothing helped them, so I recommended turn out to give the joints time to fuse. The horses would invariably come back sound."

Dr. Lewis warns, though, that not all horses are sound later, and this treatment isn't a panacea.

Lewis also urges barrel racers not to overlook the benefits of joint supplements. Products that contain chondroitin sulfate and glucosamine are often effective. "I've seen people feed it to their horses for four to six months," he says. "Then when they take them off, the horses get stiff or lame again. I've also seen some older racehorses that had undergone bone-chip surgery get better on those products, so I think they help."

Not all soreness is joint-related. For body and muscle soreness, Dr. Lewis advocates leg braces, which are cooling treatments for hot and over-worked legs. "Often, it's the little things, like leg-brace treatments, that win races. They also help you recognize when something isn't normal. You'll be surprised at what you can pick up about your horse's soundness. If you feel heat, there's a reason."

Sore suspensory ligaments are common in running horses. Often a horse with sore

TIPS

Vet-hopping

Sometimes barrel racers get so caught up in their competition schedule that when they go to a vet and he tells them, for example, to give the horse a month off to heal from an injury, they go to another vet, looking for a shortcut to healing. If they don't get the answer they want, they go to another, then another, until they finally get someone to tell them what they want to hear.

Of course, it's not a bad idea to get a second opinion on something as major as surgery. However, for everyday maintenance and most common injuries, you should listen to your regular vet who knows your horse and your program. Since he's got some history with you and your horse, he'll be the best to help you make decisions.

suspensories in both legs appears to run fine and doesn't show an obvious lameness. The only clue will be the clock; the horse won't make the times he usually does. Dr. Lewis recommends ice therapy or cold water three times a day. Also, DMSO (dimethyl sulfoxide) and aloe vera ointment or gel help, too.

Another common problem for barrel racers (and all horse owners) is colic. Dr. Lewis notes that with any colic, it's most important to get the horse on intravenous fluids right away.

Bleeders

Hard-running horses, such as racehorses and barrel horses, often bleed from their nostrils in a condition called exercise-induced pulmonary hemorrhage. Capillaries in the horse's lungs rupture and cause the bleeding. Horses with this problem often quit running because the blood runs down into their lungs and chokes them, which, in turn, scares them.

Also, they automatically slow down because they can't get enough air.

The preferred veterinary treatment is Lasix (furosemide). However, the drug is a diuretic, which is hard on kidneys. With long-term use, the kidneys wear out. They're the body's main filtering system, and they need water to work properly. However, Lasix, being a diuretic, constantly dehydrates the horse. With a kidney overload, the haircoat can turn, become rough and lose its shine.

The typical Lasix treatment is anywhere from one to five cc's. Sometimes riders who make two runs a day give two doses. For competitive barrel horses, this isn't the way to go. You'll get one or two years out of the horse that way.

If your horse coughs after he runs, there's a chance he's bleeding internally; it's just not coming out his nose. I have noticed that bleeders tend to be horses that over-exert – really gave it their all.

PHOTO BY KENNETH SPRINGER

Charmayne's uncle, Frank Brown, came to her first National Finals Rodeo (1984) and shod Scamper with shoes that allowed him to keep his footing. He had race plates with toe grabs on the front and barrel plates behind. Pictured left to right: Mary Brown (Charmayne's aunt), cousin Kelly and Frank.

Some horses bleed worse at high altitudes or in hot, humid weather. Generally, they don't bleed in the practice pen. It most likely occurs during the excitement of competition when adrenalin and blood pressure are high.

There are herbal alternatives to Lasix, which can be purchased online or from companies who sell holistic products for horses. They're administered orally, and I've had good results with some of these products in the past.

Tying-Up

Tying up (or exertional rhabdomyolysis) usually occurs shortly after beginning exercise. The most common signs are firm and painful muscles over the loin and croup areas of the topline and in the large gluteal muscles. A horse that's tying up will also usually sweat heavily, breath quick shallow breaths and have an elevated heart rate.

If your horse ties up, likely the first thing you'll notice is that he refuses to move forward. His gluteal muscles get tight, and he'll really draw up in the flanks. There are different degrees of tying up so the horse will either be so bad he can't move or he'll take only short steps behind. The condition is extremely painful, much like a giant muscle cramp.

If this happens, keep the horse still. Making him move can sometimes cause irreversible muscle damage. In bad cases, the urine will be blood-colored, indicating muscle-tissue breakdown. Call your veterinarian immediately. Treatment generally consists of tranquilizers, intravenous fluids, muscle relaxants and analgesic and anti-inflammatory drugs. The goal is to help relieve the muscle tension quickly.

Give the horse three or four days off after a tying-up episode because his hindquarter muscles are bruised and sore. If you work them too quickly, you can cause further damage.

In the past, the popular opinion was that tying-up was a feeding problem, but some horses tie up from pain or stress.

Magic tied up twice, shortly after he'd slipped and fallen. His hips and hocks were sore, and I feel he tied up from the pain.

The advice I got from fellow barrel racers was to take him off alfalfa; but he'd always been fine on alfalfa before the slip. Once he was over the initial soreness and his hips and hocks were better, he never tied up again.

It's true that some horses can't take the high protein content of alfalfa, nor too much grain. For the most part, put this type horse on a high fat diet with grass hay and exercise

him daily. Such a horse can't tolerate being kept up in a stall all the time.

For the second type of horse that ties up from pain, anything that causes them discomfort can make them stress and worry over it. Figure out where the pain is coming from and help them become as comfortable as possible.

Mares seem to be more at risk for tying up. I've known more mares than geldings who suffered from it. Those mares had feet, hock or other problems and that added to the stress of competition.

Horseshoer

Right before my first NFR, my shoer reset Scamper's shoes, instead of putting new ones on him. Back then, the theory was to leave the toe long, so the horse could reach and grab, and that's how Scamper was shod. I got to the finals and Scamper had a long toe and a worn rim shoe with very little traction.

The ground was terrible – with horses falling down every night. My Uncle Frank, a horseshoer, came to the Finals and re-shod Scamper, trimming the toe and putting on some race plates with toe grabs on the front and barrel plates behind. Scamper was able to stand up; they gave him confidence.

Think of the purpose of shoes. They're there to protect the hoof and to provide traction. It sounds simple, but there's a lot to consider. Hoofs should be trimmed correctly and at the right angles. The ideal angle is what's natural for the horse, and it should follow the angle of the pastern. The feet should be trimmed so the horse stands squarely underneath himself – not stood up too much (high-heeled), nor with too low a heel. I believe barrel horses need traction – especially rodeo horses. The ground is usually prepared and maintained better at jackpots and futurities, but seven times out of 10 the ground will be somewhat slick at rodeos.

For years, I had vets and a lot of people tell me that toe grabs would tear up Scamper's legs, and that rims would mess up his hocks. But the one thing that hurt Scamper the most was slipping. He lasted 10 years, and I really believe that traction kept him from getting hurt really bad.

I think that when horses slip out behind leaving a barrel it's because their back feet don't have traction. That can cause stifle and hip soreness, causing the horse to not stride out as he should. In subsequent runs, he might still look like he's leaving the barrel fine, but he won't stop the clock as fast because he's sore. You can't really see the difference, but it shows up in the time.

This also happens to horses that have had the toes of their rear feet squared off. The theory is that the horses can run faster

Charmayne prefers level-grip aluminum shoes with no-vibe pads on the front.

From left, the inner rim shoe has toe grabs, plus the inner rim is higher. (Charmayne uses these in front.) The middle shoe is a level-grip that goes on the front or back feet, and the Queens plate (on the right) is similar but the level grip has a slightly higher toe grab. The Queens plate can go on either the back or front.

TIPS

Horse Hoof No-No's

• Always shoe your horse. You can't control the facilities where you compete. Often, you'll have to walk across rocks or gravel, and sometimes there's nothing but pavement.

• Don't change horseshoers repeatedly. Over the years, I've seen more horses put out of competition because of a new shoer. What I did is stick with same shoers and flew them in to shoe my horses.

• Carry a set of shaped shoes for your horse. If you have to have someone tack a shoe back on, ask him to put the nails in the same holes if possible. Make sure you have someone who's reputable and knows what he's doing.

because they break over faster, but in reality you can feel them slip out behind.

I've not heard of many barrel horse injuries caused by too much traction. Most injuries seem to come, not from falling, but from slipping.

Many riders keep their horses flat shod (no traction) behind; but if a horse feels he's slipping, he'll shorten his stride to protect himself and not be as fast.

Here's an example of traction you might relate to: Think of playing on a basketball court in your socks; you'd find yourself sliding around. Put on tennis shoes with traction, and you can keep your footing. Also, traction doesn't tear up your knees. When I played basketball as a youngster, we wanted our shoes to grab, so we'd spit on them to get them to grab even better.

I'd been using steel shoes with toe grabs on Scamper for a while, when two-time All American Futurity Champion trainer James McArthur asked me, "Charmayne, would you rather run in boots or tennis shoes?"

I'd heard stories about how aluminum shoes wouldn't hold up, but he convinced me to try them on Scamper. I allowed his shoer, Charlie Williamson, to put them on and they really worked. I've used them ever since.

Traditional steel barrel racing plates have a higher rim on the outside. You can use them all the way around, but often steel wears down fast – even in a few days on concrete.

I really like to use the Queen's plate aluminum shoes behind. They have a rim outside plus reinforced steel in the toe to keep them from wearing off. In the front, I prefer the level-grip shoe because it has a slightly higher toe grab on it, which gives a good amount of traction but not too much.

Robert Treasure, of Chino, California, shod Cruiser for several years including the year we won the world championship. On Cruiser, he used an inner rim on the front with a no-vibe pad. It had a steep high rim on the inside plus a toe grab. I alternated using the Queens plate and the level grip behind.

When it comes to shaving hundredths of seconds off your time, think of every advantage for your horse. The choice between using aluminum versus steel shoes is part of the decision process. Racehorse trainers don't use steel shoes on racehorses for a reason. With aluminum, horses can run lower to the ground and stop the clock faster. There's a down-side to aluminum, though, in that some horses could have a reaction to the aluminum, but I've never had problems with them.

If you decide to go the aluminum-shoe route, be sure to use a shoer who's experienced with them. If you have a shoer who's comfortable only with steel shoes put on aluminums, they're not likely to stay on.

If you're not able to get a shoer who can put on aluminum shoes, try a rim shoe all the way around. Barrel-racing shoes are a little hard to shape, so make sure to get someone who can level the shoes well.

Aluminum shoes require small nails and that makes a big difference in keeping the foot from splitting and cracking. Speaking of nails, there are some rodeos, like the Calgary Stampede, that have horribly slick ground. Most riders put ice or mud nails in their horseshoes to help keep them on.

Some horses can wear slick shoes and still run anywhere. But the point is that if you race in bad ground, having shoes with traction helps you avoid a catastrophic slip that could hurt your horse.

Also, check regularly for loose shoes. If you get beyond six weeks on a set of shoes and the horse's toes get long, there's more strain on the tendons.

Keep in mind, however, that shoeing is only half the equation. Even the best shoe job can be stymied by a bad spot in the ground. Leg boots are so important. Probably one of the most vulnerable areas is the sesamoid bone. Splint bones seem to be a little tougher, but sesamoids can fracture and chip. Just a bruise will keep your horse out for six weeks.

More About Hoof Care

Hoof dressings are a necessity if you give daily baths to your horse. Repeated wetting and drying causes horse's hoofs to dry out. Being out on the pasture with a lot of dew is also drying. Apply the dressing on the outside of the hoof. Also, dressing doesn't allow for moisture to get in.

I packed Cruiser's feet on the bottom with a hoof-packing formula several days before Robert shod him, and then two to three times a week, depending on the climate. Dry, hard feet don't absorb as much shock as feet with some moisture in them.

I used one of the many brands of hoof packing on the market to pack Cruiser's soles. I'd cut out small pieces of brown paper and place them over the soles. Then I'd vet wrap the hoofs and secure them with duct tape. I let the horse wear this overnight. Doing this before shoeing also helps if you've a horse that gets sore after being shod.

Be aware, though, that soft feet are more susceptible to stone bruises from rocks or frozen ground.

Clean out your horse's feet daily. You never know if there's a rock or something lodged in the hoofs. This is especially important if you're in an area with rocks or gravel parking lots. Look for thrush and treat if you smell an odor.

The Chiropractor

Equine chiropractors apply the same principles of physical manipulation of the spinal column and body-structure adjustments as their human counterparts, and, in my opinion, with the same successful results.

My equine chiropractors, Scotty Wilson and his apprentice, Darrell Elliott, attend most of my barrel racing clinics. It's incredible to watch them work on the clinic horses and see how many have problems.

When they go over a horse, they begin from the head and work back, testing the usual acupressure points. According to Scotty, one of the most common situations is that the horse will be off in his neck. Usually, that's caused by the horse having set back when he was tied or put on a hot walker, or from slipping.

This type injury causes scar tissue in the neck and results in lateral stiffness in the horse. The horse ends up holding his nose out, so his rider puts a tie-down on him. Forcing him into this painful position causes more damage and makes him even more resistant.

Scotty explains, "Often, when we see this sort of neck injury, the horse has had it quite a while and learned to live with it. For example, the horse sits back, breaks a lead rope, maybe falls down. The rider checks him out. He's not lame, and there's no blood so she figures he's okay, but he's definitely not!"

One way to detect spinal problems is to watch the horse graze. If he can't touch the ground with his toes together, he's got problems.

When Scotty and Darrell adjust a horse, they do so very carefully, manipulating the horse's body into the correct position, then they adjust by hand. They also check full flexion of all joints, as well as tendons and suspensory ligaments, by testing acupressure points.

After an adjustment, most horses visibly relax. They lick their lips and blow and you can tell they feel better. When Scotty or Darrell complete an adjustment, they use a

Equine chiropractor Scotty Wilson examines a horse thoroughly before deciding what adjustments are needed.

tennis ball as a deep massage tool to stimulate the acupressure points.

Scotty also eschews the popular concept of tail pulling. "There's nothing to it. The sacrum is a solid mass of bone, and pulling the tail will not affect it."

Scotty recommends normal chiropractic maintenance about every three months, or whenever a horse is sore.

Any time a horse is sore or stiff, an adjustment will help but the horse will likely need lots of flexing and bending. In the time away from the chiropractor, it's important to do stretching exercises every day. Have your horse stretch for some hay or a treat, turning right, then left to get the treat – toward the cinch, then even farther up toward the top of the back as the horse becomes more flexible.

Scotty also recommends a lot of long-trotting. "It is great to loosen up horses; it stretches the front legs and increases the range of motion."

Acupuncture

Acupuncture is an ancient Chinese form of medicine based on the positive and negative flow of energy along meridian or acupuncture points throughout a human's or animal's body. Blockages or imbalances are rectified by stimulating the points with the exact placement of fine needles, electrical currents, laser beams or other forms of stimulation.

Acupuncture compliments the work of the chiropractor, makes adjustments last longer and helps the horse to get over the adjustment quicker.

The Dentist

Another important member of your team should be an equine dentist. I've relied on Randy Reidinger for years. He comes to all our clinics, and people are always amazed at the change in performance that comes from properly aligning the teeth and getting rid of painful mouth problems.

Randy, a former horse trainer and roper, is passionate about the importance of equine dentistry, and he's an advocate for the horses he works on.

"So many times, a rider will punish a horse when he's just trying to tell them something," explains Randy. "A horse doesn't want to bend to the right because it hurts him to do so and instead of listening, the rider ties his head around. Can you imagine how painful that is?"

A horse's mouth changes from the day the horse is born until he's 30 or so, but the period of time when the most change occurs is between the ages of two and five. For most horses, that's the time when they're in intensive

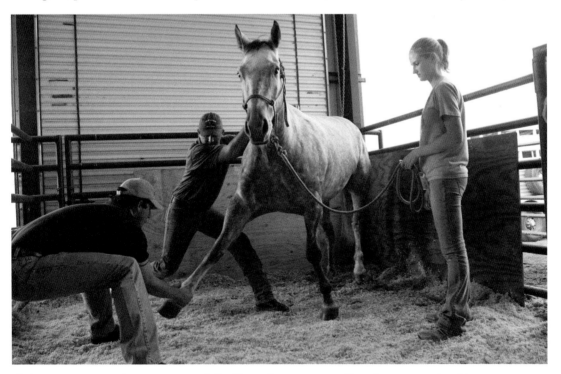

Select your equine chiropractor carefully. Since there are no uniform laws governing this treatment, skill and knowledge levels vary drastically. Darrell Elliott (left) has gone through a multi-year apprentice program with Scotty Wilson. When Wilson began, he apprenticed for many years, as well.

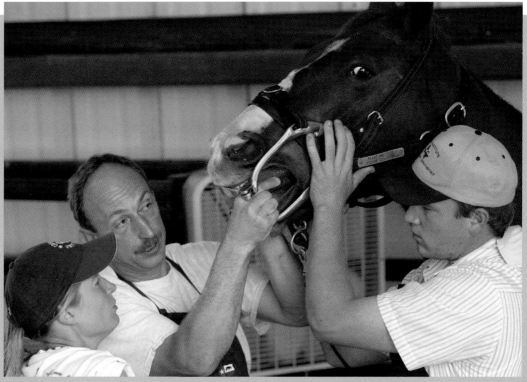

Equine dentist Randy Reidinger, center, examines a horse's mouth, using a speculum to keep the mouth open.

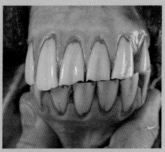

It's easy to see why this horse couldn't chew side-to-side. The uneven growth prevented proper chewing.

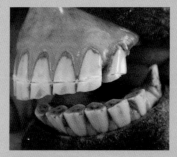

The dental correction done on the bottom teeth and marked on the top teeth will allow the horse's jaw to move properly.

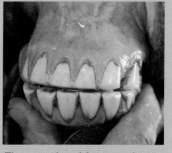

The completed front teeth give the horse a good grinding surface.

This upper hook was not only cutting the horse's mouth below, it was also pinching the cheek against the bit and not allowing the jaw to move properly.

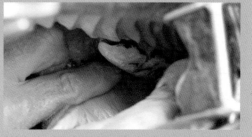

With the hook removed, the horse was able to chew better and was no longer in pain from the pressure on the gums.

training and have different types of bits in their mouths.

A horse first grows deciduous or baby teeth, then sheds them and grows permanent teeth. Through that process, a horse sheds a couple dozen teeth in the first five years of his life. Then, his permanent teeth grow for the rest of his life.

One of the reasons pasture turn-out and feeding hay are so important for the horse's health is that a horse is designed to graze with his head down 16 to 18 hours a day. In that position, his front incisors and molars are worn smooth by the grinding action of the upper and lower jaws, side-to-side and front-to-back. When you feed grain and/or processed hay (cubes or pellets) twice a day at head level or higher, you interrupt this process. With this modified position and processed food that is consumed quickly, the teeth continue to grow. However, instead of grinding with full contact, they make only partial contact. It's not unusual for the edges of the teeth to grow uninhibited. Then, sharp hooks grow so long that they cut the horse's cheeks and even the gums.

At that point, pain prevents the horse from chewing side-to-side or front-to-back, so he's only able to work his molars up and down. That further interrupts the grinding so that digestion is impaired. But equally important is the effect this has on performance. Teeth problems restrict the front to back movement of the lower jaw as the horse raises and lowers his head.

When the horse raises his head, his jaw moves back. and when he lowers his head, the jaw comes forward. If his teeth have grown to the point that they restrict this motion, and there's unequal crown height, it quickly causes the TMJ (temporomandibular joint) to become sore.

Most bridles put pressure on the lower jaw – left and right and forward and back – and that increases the horse's pain.

Besides keeping the chewing surfaces in good shape, I have my dentist create bit seats on all my riding horses – that refers to the rounding and lowering of the first pre-molars of the upper and lower jaws. Changing this surface from the natural cornered edge keeps the horse's lips and tongue from getting squeezed or cut between the bit and the tooth corner.

Have your equine dentist check your horse's mouth at least twice yearly. Keeping on top of dental problems is the best way to avoid them.

Barrel races are won by horses – each an individual with its own personality, sensitivities, strengths and weaknesses.

12

THE HORSES

Profiled in this chapter are the horses that were prominent in my career. Reading about them, you'll likely see some similarities with your own horses.

Bardo Deck

1974 sorrel Quarter Horse gelding by Central Deck (by War Deck) out of Barbarda by Quick M Silver

"Bardo"

At over 16 hands, Bardo Deck was a sorrel Thoroughbred-looking Appendix Quarter Horse that had been run on the track. My parents bought him for my oldest sister, Eugenie, who eventually married, moved away and didn't want him. The horse I was riding had foot problems so I constantly asked my parents to let me ride Bardo, and they kept telling me that he was too much horse.

Finally they let me ride him. My Dad put a Sliester high-port bit on him so he wouldn't take off with me because I was so little. The first day, he was a mess. I worked cattle on him, and he'd run sideways. I was scared to death but didn't let my parents know. By the end of the day, the two of us got better and I liked him.

That summer (1979) I rode him all day, everyday and we bonded. Bardo wasn't very well broke and he was extremely high-strung, but by the time I'd ridden him day after day, I became friends with him and he rode much better. My family took us to open rodeos, where I won about $15,000 on him in two summers. He was five and I was nine.

He always worked very well in big, outdoor arenas on hard ground. When I rode him indoors at a big barrel race in Abilene, Texas, however, he knocked down barrels both runs because he'd never run in a building before. I knew then that I had to run him in more buildings.

Looking back on it, I've come to realize that Bardo was the kind of horse that needed lots of riding. I was just a kid and had never been exposed to any kind of barrel racing techniques, or good riding basics, such as walking, flexing, bending to inside, etc., so when I started him on barrels I simply took him around the barrels over and over. Riding him so many hours each day is what made the difference.

Back then, I wasn't aware of leads, but because I rode two-handed and my father taught me to ride with light hands, Bardo stayed collected with his back end up under him. I guided him where I wanted to go and never pulled on him.

The second summer I rode Bardo, my sister, Bernadette, borrowed him for a high school rodeo. She was going to run barrels and poles so she hauled him downtown to the Clayton (New Mexico) arena to make a practice run on him. He stepped in a hole and broke his leg.

We hauled him to the veterinary hospital in Raton, New Mexico, where the vets put a cast on him. They suggested, however, that we take him to the vet school at Colorado State University in Fort Collins. When the vets

Charymayne and Bardo won $15,000 in two summers of barrel racing.

Scamper in 2005 at age 28.

Probably the most unforgettable run in barrel racing history – Charmayne and Scamper in the seventh round at the 1985 NFR. A broken bridle doesn't hinder their winning time of :14.40.

Charmayne James :14.40 1st Place $5,050.00 7th Go 1985 NFR Las Vegas, Nev. Dec. 13th

PHOTO BY SPRINGER

The little-known second run while losing a bridle happened at Yuma, Colorado, in 1989.

PHOTO BY SHANNA NEWLAND

there examined him, they said he had to be put down.

Even now, looking back, it was traumatic. I would've done anything to save my best friend. The whole family cried when we had to put him down.

Gills Bay Boy

1977 bay Quarter Horse gelding by Gill's Sonny Boy (by Sonny GH) out of Jo Drapers Jay by Headed West

"Scamper"

After losing Bardo, my family searched for another horse for me. We checked out the race-track, but didn't find anything. Dad had his eye

on a bay gelding in his feedlot. His name was Gills Bay Boy, but we called him "Scamper."

Dad had me get on him, but told me not to lope him for 15 minutes or he'd buck me off. My mom cringed, but, by the same token, knew I'd gotten along fine on some other horses that were tough to ride.

I walked him around, then went behind the barn and kicked him into a lope. Sure enough he bucked. I kind of giggled and thought it was funny, and I think Scamper did, too. That was the start of our bonding.

Scamper had had several owners by the time he was four. He'd gone through various auctions, such as the ones in La Junta,

Barrel Racing Moments

Making a Run with the Greatest Barrel Horse Ever – 10-Time World Champion Scamper

It's getting close. I have to get somewhere near the alley. Once he feels me get ready and I start moving ahead, he'll want to lunge and take off. I've got to get up a little closer to get a good start, but not all the way to the timer. He can run the distance. I don't want anything to break his momentum to the first barrel. I want a straight shot to my position at the first barrel and the faster and harder I run him to the first barrel, the better the run will be.

He always hits on his front end. I have to make sure I'm sitting down so he won't pop me up out of the saddle going to the first barrel. If my timing isn't just perfect with his stride, he can really send me sailing. But because he's a little front-endy, it helps him handle a lot of ground. He doesn't rely on his back end only. He uses his entire body for the run. I sometimes whip on the way to the first, then put the whip in my mouth or carry it in my hand. I ride him two-handed around the barrel, and I just push my reins right up his neck, not pull him. My hand is a guide. If he gets too close to the barrel, I just put my hand farther up toward his ears.

After the first barrel, I ride as hard as I can through the rest of the run. Going to the second, I ride right to the position for the turn, never looking at the barrel, looking at the ground right where I need to go. Scamper is extremely quick around the barrels, and he's able to take three deliberate strides in making a turn. I ride him all the way to the turn and sit down just at the turn – ride him through his rating area. If I don't ride him aggressively, he shuts down too early. I ride one-handed around the second and third barrels and have the whip in my hand and my hand on the horn to settle in the turn.

Between the barrels I have the whip in one hand, and the other hand on the reins. If I use the whip he responds well. He likes to look around a lot and is kind of spooky so he pays attention better if I carry the whip. By the way, the whip has a popper; it's not one that stings him.

Riding stride for stride all the way around barrel three, my next objective is to get across the timer without him shutting down. I pick a spot past the timer and run to it. When I've gotten past the timer, I stand in the stirrups and ask him to trickle down and leave the arena.

In the second go of the 1986 NFR in Las Vegas, Charmayne and Scamper ran third in :14.02.

PHOTO BY SPRINGER

Colorado; Guyman, Oklahoma; Clovis, New Mexico, and Clayton, New Mexico. After the Clayton sale, he was purchased by Ron Holland, a cowboy in our feedlot.

Somewhere along the line, he'd gotten really well broke. When I tried him out, he'd slide to a stop, spin, pick up his leads and change leads. He was soft in the poll and so broke I was able to lope him around the barrels the very first day.

Two weeks after I started him around the barrels that summer, I took him to a jackpot in Texline, Texas. We won the juniors and ran the third fastest time in the open.

I rode him in a Tom Thumb snaffle for some time at the amateur rodeos. He won money everywhere, and each time we ran he got better.

Scamper was never a deadhead but neither was he one to prance around and be nervous. He was always quiet in the beginning until he figured it was time to run. Then he became a

ball of energy. From the start, he'd go into an arena and hunt barrels.

The ground at a lot of the rodeos wasn't good, but I think his feedlot background helped him stand up in a lot of places with bad ground.

As time went on, he got to where he'd get away from me in the alley. Dad put a grazing bit on him. This low-port bit had a solid mouthpiece with reasonably short shanks that curved slightly back. Scamper went well in that for a while, then he started to get away from me again. I was about 12 when Dad changed to a Sliester bit on him. It had a solid mouthpiece with a high port and shanks. It seemed to work well. There were some rodeos I remember him running past the first barrel some, but we seldom knocked over barrels in those amateur rodeo days.

A friend told my parents I should get my professional card and try to win Women's Pro

Magic liked the mud, and he won the Calgary Stampede in a lot of it!

Rodeo Rookie of the Year. My first professional rodeo was in Raton, New Mexico. Scamper saw some bulls in the chute at the second barrel and ducked off because he wasn't used to seeing bulls there.

In 1983, we won the pro rodeo in Dodge City, Kansas, where I won enough money to fill my permit. I bought a card in November and went to the Kansas City Royale PRCA Rodeo in Kansas City, Kansas, where we knocked down a barrel one run and placed in another. It was intermittent like that until I got my head together the first of the year and won the Houston Livestock Show and Rodeo. From then on Scamper learned how to handle the rodeos more and more.

I spent a lot of time with Scamper from the very beginning. We lived on the feedlot, and my daily schedule was riding and helping the cowboys. When my parents built a house away from the lot, I'd ride him around the wheat fields near the house after I'd get home from school. I'd start out by walking and trotting and then graduating to a lope. This took about 45 minutes or an hour. In the beginning I'd make a run three to four times a week. I'd do everything on him, then make a run and quit. When I did that, he was a lot sharper at rodeos.

I rode or exercised Scamper every day, even in bad weather. I might keep his blankets on but I still got him out every day. In the summer when it was hot, I'd get on him bareback and ride through the sprinklers in the wheat fields. He loved it.

During the 1984 National Finals Rodeo Scamper came down with a respiratory infection, and we had to leave him at a vet clinic for two weeks right after the Finals. The vet devised an oxygen mask for him, which consisted of a nebulizer and a breathing mask. In the beginning he breathed oxygen mixed with saline and antibiotics. Later, he had oxygen with only saline, which encouraged him to cough up the congestion before we ran. Because this helped him so much, I carried an oxygen tank and always gave him breathing treatments before I ran.

Scamper was really mean to other horses. I couldn't tie him near other horses because he'd kick or bite them. He liked only whatever buddy horse that hauled with him.

Scamper made probably the most famous barrel run of all time at the 1985 National Finals Rodeo in the seventh round. The historic day was Friday, the 13th.

As we came through the alleyway, he hit his head on the side of the wall and must have broken the top of the Chicago screw on his headstall.

He lunged and went into the arena, and all he had was the bit in his mouth. I remember thinking to myself, "Don't panic" on the way to the first barrel. My thought was to try to keep everything picked up so he didn't step on it and hurt his mouth.

Scamper was a horse that didn't wait for a pull around the barrels – he went on the feel of my body more than anything. It was never about pulling him around the barrels. So it didn't matter when one factor of communication was gone because I didn't change the way I sat and rode. I locked on to my position and didn't veer from the barrel pattern.

And it worked. He turned the first barrel, then the second, then by the third barrel he'd spit out the bit. I tried to keep my body position normal and keep everything from falling down and tripping him.

As I headed out of the alleyway, he began to pick up more speed and he seemed to panic, figuring out that something was wrong. The guys working the gate in the back saw what was happening and started to close it. They got it almost closed but there was an opening just wide enough for Scamper and me to run through and he did because there was no stopping him at that point.

The alleyway was very long, thank goodness, and it allowed people to get in front of him and slow him down.

By the time we reached the top of the alleyway, my uncle had grabbed on to his neck and was able to bring him to a stop.

I was surprised a few minutes later when they came to get me to tell me I won the go. I never thought I would've won that round with something like that happening.

Interestingly, running without a bridle happened a second time. Scamper's headstall broke at Yuma, Colorado, in 1989. He held the bit in his mouth until after the second barrel. Around the third and on the way home, he had nothing in his mouth. We won that rodeo, too.

Bold Bars Top Man

1986 bay tovero Paint Horse gelding by Flit Bars Top Man and out of Bold Chickadee
"Magic"

Magic was six when I bought him, and it was the first time I'd ever spent a lot of money for a horse – $30,000. Janie Proffer owned him and Larry Stevens had trained him and showed him to me when I went to try him. I had called Larry and told him I wanted something young. I thought so much of Larry that anything he'd ridden and trained was probably good enough for me. He told me about Magic, who'd placed at futurities and derbies.

This was really the first time I had been on a barrel horse someone else had trained. Our styles weren't the same, so I had to learn to adjust to Magic. I wasn't used to picking up and holding the inside rein. I'd always given my horses the reins and that wasn't a good thing to do on Magic. The first time I went a stride past the first barrel because I hadn't picked him up. The next run, my timing was better, and we had a nice run.

I really liked him and felt I could get with him and he'd teach me a lot. It took a while but finally I got where I could be consistent on him.

To make a run on him, I'd hand-walk him before the run to keep him from getting nervous. I'd get on him when there were about four

PHOTO BY FAIN

Magic had a lot of try, even when the ground wasn't good. This photo really gives you an idea of what rodeo horses have to go through, as far as ground, and what the wear and tear can be like on their legs.

or five runners to go. I'd stand next to a buddy horse or whoever I was traveling with would get on a horse and ride with me to the alley to keep him as quiet as possible. I had to find the perfect winning speed going to the first barrel.

In the beginning, if we went too fast or too slow we'd go by the barrel. This is where I had to work on my timing and picking the perfect speed.

Going to the first, I had to keep a little hold on him – not a tight grip – but I couldn't let him run free either. Then I'd sit down, pick up and drop the outside rein for the turn when I felt the time was right.

I could really feel his power. He'd set on his hind end and come back very hard, kind of like a rollback. He was fun to ride, but initially I had to be perfect because of the tight rollback.

Magic had a rollback-style of running barrels. That meant that he had more of a "vee" turn around the barrels, and, when a horse vees, you can hit the barrel coming in and coming out.

I watched tapes on both Magic and Scamper. I figured out that Magic needed to take more steps around the barrel instead of just going in and out. I practiced loping around the barrels and got him to where I didn't have to pull on him. He rounded out around the barrels and got real solid so I didn't hit many barrels any more.

I really had to concentrate at first, then finally my muscle memory took over. Eventually, my timing got better, and I was able to ride two-handed to get him to turn more rounded. He was smooth around barrels and used his hindquarters more than Scamper.

Magic was a free-runner to the second so I could basically sit on him and let him run. He'd get in a little tight at the second and third. If he got too tight, I really had to lift the reins to keep him off the barrels.

In the beginning, because I tried to stay quiet, I rode him one-handed between the barrels. Then, I found that with two hands I could hold the position better going to the second and the third.

As Magic got older, I had to hustle him. He got more round around the barrel and had more rate. Once he turned the third, he was a free-runner all the way home and stopped fine.

Early in our career together, when I did run, I'd make one good run out of 10. I could make perfect practice runs all day long, but I had to learn to make them at the rodeos.

Magic ended up being really good in arenas where we had to go in and set up (in arenas with no center alley, you have to ride into the arena and go across to your starting point to begin the run). He was also good about running to a closed gate. In this regard Magic was very different than Scamper who didn't like side gates and running to a closed gate on the way back from third barrel. Also, Magic loved to run in the mud and Scamper hated it.

Initially, I rode Magic in a smooth, medium-shank snaffle (jointed or broken mouthpiece) and a tie-down. But before long, I moved him into a broken bit with a port (correctional, which is a jointed mouthpiece with hinged port in the middle) and loose-jawed shanks and took off the tie-down.

He was very high-strung. If you tied him to the trailer, he'd stand on the running board, or paw and rear up.

When I went to rodeos, he wanted to jig and prance and look at every thing. I just did my best to keep him quiet. I'd walk him – then get off – then walk.

I kept him away from nervous horses and nervous people.

1993 was the year of the tenth world title with Scamper. I had to use Magic that year at the Finals because Scamper had gotten a viral infection and his red blood count dropped. I opted to let him sit out a run. When I got on Magic for that one run, I knew I had to make a solid run and keep the barrels up. Having had him two years allowed me to have the confidence in him to do that.

A lot of people didn't give Magic enough credit, in my opinion. His first year on his own at the 1994 NFR, I didn't win much on him. I had tried to win the Dodge truck that year. I went from California to Montana to Texas to Florida and back to California. He caught the flu after that trip, and just didn't recuperate by the NFR.

Even though I did win about $250,000 on him, I'd hear, "He ain't no Scamper." Well, obviously, but in my life he was great. He taught me so much about timing and about learning the ways of another horse. You get one horse you win on and expect other horses to run exactly the same. Scamper and Magic were opposites, and I was proud Magic and I finally got together.

I ended up selling him once I knew I had Cruiser coming along. Also, I was in a situation where I wanted to start my dream of a horse ranch, so I sold him and bought some broodmares.

Slewparonion

1991 sorrel Quarter Horse gelding by Cameronian (by Dash For Cash) out of Charm O Swade by Go Swade Go
"Slewpy"

Slewpy was six when my partner, Neil Gibson, and I bought him together from Marion Grammith of Stephenville, Texas. She had placed on him at some of the futurities, and I thought the big (15.3 hand) sorrel gelding had potential.

Even though he had some soundness problems in the front end, Neal and I thought we could keep him together. He rode great the day I tried him, but he hadn't been to any rodeos. I started hauling him in May and June of 1997, but it was three months before I won anything on him. By the end of the year, I started to figure out timing with him and that was important. He was such a free-runner that timing had to be just perfect.

Before we got ready to make a run, I'd have him stand or walk quietly to keep him relaxed. When they called for me I'd move him into the alley and feel him get a little nervous as we approached the in-gate. I wanted to have his nose tipped slightly to the inside, which kept him shaped before we took off. When I did go, I held him with a light hold to keep him at a controlled speed. Going to the first barrel, I had to time picking up on him perfectly. It wasn't always the same because of the arena size or ground. It's just a feel you have to develop. A horse has to be committed to turn. You're locked on; he's locked in.

Slewpy worked more off his hind end than Scamper, so he was very smooth around the barrel. Once around the first, I could bear down and ride him a little harder.

In the beginning, he would fade into the second and third barrels, so I'd guide him into position with both reins to keep from hitting them. Going to the third, I'd hold my outside rein a little longer. I continued to ride him in the correct position and with time he became more solid.

In the turns my hand was there as a guide unless I had to pick him up. Going to the third I hustled him and bumped with my legs, urging him forward, but not quite as aggressively

Slewpy won this go at the 1997 National Finals Rodeo.

as with Scamper. I rode him one-handed in all three turns and two-handed in between.

I'd ride him hard coming out because he was good about stopping at the end of the pattern – even when the arena gate was open. Even so, I'd stop him gradually to reduce the wear and tear on his legs.

I rode him in a bit with a broken twisted-wire mouthpiece with a medium shank. Marion had ridden him in a wire tie-down, and I left that on initially because that was what he was used to going in. I ended up changing him to a leather tie-down. I felt he had a lot of response in that bridle, and that's what I left on him.

Slewpy was a quiet horse, but he could get spooky, so the quieter and more relaxed I could keep him, the better, especially going up the alley. When he took off, it had to be a perfect speed that was controlled instead of an all-out run. I didn't hold him up, but we also didn't go Mach 10. I wouldn't lean far forward either. I'd keep body movement real slow when I was ready to take off.

I had to tell myself that slower was faster. The slower I went on him, the faster I was. If I tried to hurry, the run would turn out a little too wild to stop the clock. When I slowed everything down, that's when we were smooth and won and that's when he had the fastest time.

I qualified for the 1997 NFR on him, and he ran the fastest time of the finals that year. He slipped in one of the early goes, tore a muscle and got really sore so we didn't do well the rest of the week.

Maintenance for Slewpy was to give him exercise every day. I mostly walked or trotted around the barrels – no runs. I mainly kept him ridden.

I rode him only that one year, then sold him to Betty Becham when I knew I had Cruiser coming along and doing well.

Cruisen On Six

1991 sorrel Quarter Horse gelding by Streakin Six (by Easy Six) out of Moon Cruisin by Master Hand (TB)

"Cruiser"

I bought Cruiser in 1994 at the Clovis horse sale as a 3-year-old. He was by Streakin Six and out of a Master Hand-Lady Bugs Moon mare on the bottom. He was in a pen with five or six other horses, so Mom and I climbed over the fence to see him. He pinned his ears and ran us out of there!

He hadn't been cataloged for the sale but was going to be run through it as a supplemental (additional) consignment. We found the people who had consigned him, and they allowed me to ride him before the sale. It was like riding a rubber band, but I could tell he had a lot of athletic ability. I bought him before the sale for $2,000. He was thin, long-haired, and scrawny, but had good legs and feet and great breeding.

Cruiser had been to the racetrack and was unproven as an early 2-year-old. The owner put him with a cutting horse trainer for 30 days because he wanted to keep him as a riding horse. But then decided he wouldn't be a good riding horse, either, because he was very spooky.

When I bought him, I had Magic and Scamper, so Cruiser was a project to play with on the side. From the first day I put him on the barrels, he really watched them. Because I was hauling the other two horses, I rode Cruiser when I could and only occasionally took him with me. I had a friend ride him on a ranch, working cattle on him, and he absolutely hated Cruiser because he was so spooky and didn't ride well.

Cruiser didn't get a lot of barrel work for the first couple of years. I just tried to get him broke so he was a little easier to ride. I'd rope on him or run cattle out of the arena.

In 1996 I worked him on barrels, but he still wasn't to the point of being able to go to a jackpot.

In 1998, I started bearing down on him around the barrels. I took him to his first jackpot in March. He won the Under $2K class (a division where the horse cannot have won $2,000 in his career). When he ran in, he looked at everything and zigzagged five times on the way to the first barrel, but, when he got there, he turned. He zigzagged to the second and third, as well, but he could fly and was just so quick in his turns.

I then took him to a couple of rodeos, and he didn't do too badly. I was very close to placing on him. We did place in April at a PRCA rodeo in Logandale, Nevada. It was his third or fourth pro rodeo.

At the Laughlin Stampede PRCA Rodeo in Laughlin, Nevada, he turned in front of the second barrel when he got scared of the arena banners, but I already knew this horse had great potential and loved running barrels.

The problem was, he was so high strung and looked at everything. He turned well, but he'd

Cruiser's solid conformation and blinding speed took Charmayne to her 11th world championship.

get to running so fast that I had to slow him up. I started out riding him in a twisted-wire gag bit. He was really bendy and flexible, so I rode him two-handed to keep him gathered. Even though I hadn't competed on him until March, I won enough money on him that year to qualify for the NFR.

At the NFR practice run, he saw the camera pit as he ran in and didn't even notice that there was a first barrel. Needless to say, I was nervous.

Then, he was so afraid of the stagecoach that was part of grand entry that Sue Miller had to come over and help me saddle. We had to hold up one of his legs to get him saddled. That's how scared he was!

He never did get completely relaxed, but he got better. That night he worked well and went around the barrels just fine. He won the last two rounds and we earned $65,000, just nine months after his first jackpot.

After the NFR, I moved him up to a broken bit with a little longer shank, and he wasn't quite as bendy in it. From there, we went to a long-shank three-piece Quick bit, then to a Sliester low port.

Even when he was wound up and looking around, he always went into the arena and worked. It might not have been pretty and he might have gone a half stride past, but he was

so fast he could make it up. I felt he would get more solid.

I knew he was going to make mistakes, but I didn't get after him. A lot of people thought he was so radical, but he had a lot to deal with as green as he was.

Every run was a new run, and I had to react. Cruiser never had a problem as far as hitting the barrels, but I never knew what he was going to look at. I can remember him running to the third at the NFR and looking up into the stands. I thought, "Well, he's done this before and still turned it" and he did.

But it's disconcerting knowing your horse isn't locked in.

He could change directions so fast that I knew I'd better hang on. He loved it and was fun to run barrels on. 1998 was my first year on him. I rode him until I retired from rodeoing full-time in 2003.

Making a run on Cruiser was fun; getting ready was a challenge. He was ornery at the stall or trailer. It was kind of like a game. He'd pin his ears and stomp his foot. I was around him so long it didn't bother me.

To get ready for a run, I would ride him, but at times he'd prance and jig and spook so much that I couldn't lope him. At home he was fine and I could rope on him, but when he'd get away from home, he was very nervous.

Cruiser and Charmayne at the 1999 NFR.

Charmayne and Boomer at the 2000 NFR.

Sometimes I warmed him up on a longe line so he'd stay quieter. At some rodeos, like the San Antonio Livestock Show, it's loud behind the chutes because they load trucks in and out with rodeo stock. In that environment he knew it was rodeo time, and I had to keep him walking and as quiet as possible so he could focus.

When I was ready to go, I'd sit on him a couple of horses before our turn, trying to keep him as quiet as I could, moving to the alleyway and as close to the eye (timer) as possible. He was easy to hold in the alley. I didn't let him run full speed to the first. I let him run at a good, controlled speed. I rode two-handed to the first and all the way around for the first several years.

He never rated a lot. He'd run in fast and switch directions going really fast. It was extremely difficult to keep my balance on him because he'd zigzag instead of running straight. He was bendy and "waspy" and might not do the same thing twice. In the years I ran him, there were maybe 10 rodeos where he made flawless runs, but he was so fast he could still win even in the difficult runs.

Cruiser was a free-runner so I seldom kicked him going to the first barrel; I just pushed my hands forward asking him to run in between the barrels. As we got to the second, I rode two-handed all the way around because in the beginning he'd lose control of his back end. I'd ride two-handed around the third as well.

The last couple of years I got to where I didn't have to guide as much. I could ride him going two-handed to the barrel and one-handed around. I went to one hand around

PHOTO BY MIKE COPEMAN

the second and third barrel long before I went to one hand around the first.

Cruiser had a good third barrel, then he'd run hard. He was awesome in the little arenas where the timer was set inside, and you had to stop at the gate. He had no "cheat." He'd run just as hard the tenth run as he did the first run, and he stopped fine coming out.

FQH A Sharp Move

1995 sorrel Quarter Horse gelding by Sharp Rodney (by A Sharp Leo) out of Lady Bugs Move by Lady Bug's Moon.

"Boomer"

Cruiser had gotten sick after the PRCA Winter Tour Finale in Las Vegas, Nevada, so I leased Boomer from Charlie Cole in July till the end of the year to alternate the runs between the two horses.

Boomer was five, stood about 15.1 hands and hadn't been hauled much when I first started riding him, but, from riding Slewpy and Magic, I knew how to help him with his timing and confidence.

He was one I tried to keep real quiet before I ran. When I got him I was told he'd refuse to go into the arena. I kept him quiet and stayed away from the arena until it was my turn. Then, I'd wait until the arena was completely clear before moving to the alley because I didn't want to get there and have to stop and wait.

I'd walk up to the in-gate slowly and quietly, with one hand on the reins. When we were in position I'd put two hands on the reins and tip his nose to the inside as we took off. Then, when we got to the turn, I'd pick up on the inside rein and twist my wrist slightly. I couldn't just run in there and pull on him.

Boomer was a real free-running horse. He worked on his rear and was really smooth. He never got tight on the barrels and always stayed shaped. I'd go to the second with two hands, then I'd drop to one around the barrel. I had to sit down and pick up with a guiding hold while keeping his nose tipped slightly to the inside all the way around. I'd ride him quiet going to the third. Depending on how much he was running was how much I'd get after him. At the third, I'd sit down, pick up his nose slightly to the inside then hustle him out. He stopped great coming out.

We won the PRCA rodeo at Williams Lake, British Columbia, and were second at the Ponoka, Alberta, PRCA rodeo, and second at the Lewiston, Idaho PRCA Tour rodeo. I'd

never won Cheyenne Frontier Days before, but I did on Boomer and placed at several other big rodeos. It was amazing that he was just a five-year-old. I just loved that horse.

He had some coffin bone problems and a hock problem so I could run him only so often. I'd pick and choose the places to run, then lay him off a week.

Boomer ran in a light hackamore noseband. I took him to the NFR that year. In the lease contract, his owners got to take him to the All American Quarter Horse Congress in Columbus, Ohio, where they ran poles on him. He unfortunately slipped and got real sore.

I went into the NFR with a chance to win the world. I had two great horses, but they were both sore before it was over. Boomer was sore from the Congress, and Cruiser slipped in one of the rounds and got sore.

Dash Dreamer

1996 bay Quarter Horse gelding by Black Dash (by Streakin Six) out of Crystal Fatima by Zircon

"Sea Doo"

I bought Sea Doo as a three-year-old in 1999. My parents were friends with the people who had him, and I really liked his breeding. He was a tall, lanky colt – real racy, about 15.1 at the time, very quiet and easy going.

PHOTO BY SPRINGER

Sea Doo has been one of the most challenging horses for Charmayne, but she feels he's so fast and talented that his idiosyncracies are worth working around.

He had maybe 30 days of riding on him when I got him. For the first two years I rode him in the pasture and arena and hauled him to some rodeos. I started him by walking and trotting around the barrels, then I turned him out in the pasture. All along he seemed quiet and laid back and seemed to work better the more we worked him.

As we progressed, I started to ask for more handle and speed, and he did really well but was funny about his head. I couldn't find the right bridle for him. He'd shake his head, so I kept a ring snaffle on him.

I sent him to my dad to ride because I wanted to get him broke better. At that point, I was at the stage of loping barrels fast and knew that if I went faster, he might not hold together.

Dad, who's a wonderful horseman with great hands, had Sea Doo six months during his five-year-old year. Working cattle with Sea Doo at the feedlot, he got along with him great. He got him more broke and did him a lot of good, but Sea Doo still shook his head.

I let my friend Johnette Norris ride him for a while. Johnette knew he had a head-shaking problem so she did all she could not to touch him. He basically did fine around the barrels if you didn't touch him. Then, one time he came out of the arena running too fast, and because of his head-shaking, she didn't want to pick up on him at first. When she finally did, nothing happened. That's when he started running off coming out of the arena.

I had had dental work done on Sea Doo in the past, but when my equine dentist Randy Reidinger checked him, he found and corrected some real problems that had likely been the source of the head-shaking. Unfortunately, even when his mouth was fixed, he still had memories that would take a long time to get past.

My Dad had ridden Sea Doo in a long-shank Sliester, and he got along well with him in the feedlot, but Sea Doo didn't work barrels well in it. He seemed to do the best in a three-piece ring snaffle.

The problem with Sea Doo was that the bits that he felt comfortable running in wouldn't stop him coming out of the arena. Likewise, if you had enough bit to stop him coming out, he wouldn't work the barrels as well.

Sea Doo started winning consistently in 2004. He's run the fastest time at some of the larger jackpots, but he's still a challenge and still shakes his head sometimes. He might always do that to some degree.

He's a very free-runner. He has so much speed that it almost scares him when he gets running super fast. He can literally high lope through the barrels and still have the fastest time. It's great to see one with so much potential. At this point in his career, we're just taking our time.

Of all the horses I've ridden, however, Sea Doo is the most challenging. He wants to do so much on his own, but he's the perfect example of how the good ones often have something quirky about them. You've got to find a way to make it work. It's not always about controlling them but finding a way to work with them that they can tolerate.

When Sea Doo makes mistakes, I know I have work ahead of me if he's ever going to run barrels consistently. He's got so much potential that I'm willing to be patient with him, and that's really my only option. If I were to try to cheat him through, I don't think he could take it.

Before a run, I walk Sea Doo and constantly flex his neck making him give his nose to the inside. I walk him down a fence and pick up one rein and ask him to come back down the fence. This seems to calm him. When it's time to run, I walk with one hand on the reins as far up as I can get to the timer. When I pick up two reins on him to take off, he knows it's time to go. Sometimes, he gets a little smart and wants to take off before I'm ready so I work on control with one rein.

Out of the gate, it basically feels like I'm high-loping him to the first barrel because I want a controlled approach. I ride two-handed to the first then, when the time is right, I sit down and go to one hand. I pick him up only to shape him, and try to guide him softly.

I go two-handed to the second and let him run. I ask him to run but I don't ride aggressively because I need to ride him quietly for his long-term good.

At the second, I sit down and once again use my inside hand for a guide.

Going to the third, he sometimes wants to get in a little tight. If he does, I bump with the outside rein. When I leave the third barrel, he turns on the jets and flies home.

If there's a gate there, he slides to a stop. If there's not gate, I make sure I stop him down the fence by picking up with one rein. I never pull straight back with both reins to stop him.

A Black Feature

1987 black Quarter Horse stallion by Frosty Feature (by Truckle Feature) out of Miss Toady Jack by Sandy Jack Jordan

"Bigelow"

I bought Bigelow as a two-year-old from Bob Jordan of South Dakota. I'd been looking for some colts to start. Bigelow has a perfectly proportioned body, great legs and feet and is a beautiful mover. He really watched me as I was looking at him. I fell in love with him.

I got him used to the saddle before sending him out to have him started. He came home after 60 days, and I rode him whenever I was home, in between rodeos.

I decided to leave him a stallion because I had purchased some mares and thought he was so good-minded and good-natured that he would be a good cross on them.

Even though I planned to breed him, he wasn't kept in a stall by himself away from other horses. I left him out in the pasture with the geldings until he was four. One horse was the "alpha" horse, and Bigelow was right below him in the herd pecking order. He learned discipline from an older horse so he's never been a problem to haul.

Since he was so calm and quiet, I started hauling him to rodeos. The first time I took him in an exhibition it was like he'd done it every day of his life. He really hunted the barrels.

I took Bigelow to jackpots as a six-year-old in 2003. I ran him at the pro rodeo in Auburn, California, and he won second there. Cruiser had surgery, so I got on Bigelow and rode him at half a dozen rodeos. We were just off the pace a couple of tenths at those rodeos. He did very well to be as inexperienced as he was.

His style was to have a lot of rate around the barrels. He really turned the barrels tight. He probably worked in deeper ground better just because that's what he was used to at my place.

In the beginning I ran two-handed, but I was able to ride one hand at the barrels and ride two-handed between.

Bigelow would let you go in whatever way you wanted. However, he didn't like to walk. He'd jig, but he was very controllable. Coming out, he stopped great.

Once he was out of a snaffle, I put him in a gag bit but he tended to have too much bend with that. I put him in a solid mouthpiece bit with a port and roller. He really liked that, and it kept him really quick in his turns..

A lot of the characteristics I liked about this horse are being passed on to his foals. I've started some of them, and he's given them the same confidence and ability to focus.

Glance At Me Right

1987 brown Quarter Horse mare by You Alright (by Alamitos Bar) out of Stones Kip by Tomholme (TB)

"Glancy"

I bought Glancy after the 1994 National Finals Rodeo. Magic had gotten the flu in November, and even though we got through the finals he still wasn't on the top of his game. I thought I'd ride her until Magic got back on his feet.

She was eight when I bought her from Sharon Gunter, and had just been to a few rodeos. I didn't think she would be a world champion, but I did think she would be able to run where I wanted to go.

Glancy is about 15 hands and built like a tank. She looked like she had a lot of potential, and when I got on her she fit me. I felt that I'd be able to ride her well from day one.

I ran Glancy at the California Circuit Finals and won that, then placed at the Sand Hills Livestock Show and PRCA Rodeo in Odessa, Texas, on her.

She had a "ratey" style – you had to keep her nose tipped to the inside all the way around and hustle her to the barrels. If you didn't, she would tend to flatten her ribs. If you kept her nose tipped, it helped her keep her body shaped.

She had no bad habits, but I didn't know, when I bought her, that she was a bleeder. She bled a couple of times, and I didn't want to give her Lasix so I opted for an herbal blend that ended up working well.

When Magic was ready to go again, I sold her to Vicki Reinhart, who made the Texas Circuit Finals on her. Glancy has continued to win.

All horses and riders are different, but there are common mistakes and situations that prevent them from performing their best.

13

COMMON PROBLEMS

This chapter presents composite examples of typical horse and rider problems that I've run into at my barrel racing/horsemanship clinics. I offer workable solutions that could help you if you have similar challenges. Do you recognize yourself or your horse in any of these scenarios?

Ashley

Ashley was 11 when she came to one of my clinics. As I watched her first run, I saw that her horse was on the incorrect lead going to the first barrel. As she approached the barrel, her horse didn't switch to the correct lead. He also went past the barrel about two strides. As he began the turn he changed leads in front but not behind.

Charmayne enjoys giving back to the barrel horse industry through her clinics, and she's committed to the success of her students.

Ashley had been taught to put her hand down and pull her horse around. Her second and third barrels weren't smooth – not bad, but just not smooth. She leaned to the inside, pulled down and looked at the barrel.

When I rode her horse, I could make him pick up his left lead but not his right. When I asked him to flex to the right and left, he had some problems to the right. I immediately sent him over to Randy Reidinger, our equine dentist, who attends my clinics. Randy found some major problems in the horse's mouth – some high teeth in the back, which kept his jaw from moving properly, and some sores in the side of his jaw caused by sharp teeth.

Then, I sent him to Scotty Wilson, our chiropractor, to rule out any body soreness that might cause him to not pick up the lead, but Scotty found nothing wrong with him.

When I got back on the horse, I asked him to turn his head to one side, then the other, to let him get the feel of his new mouth. When I loped him, he was willing to take the lead right away. I could stop him, cue him back into a lope and he'd pick up the right lead immediately. The improvement was that fast!

I loped him through the barrels a few times, very light-handed, riding him in correct position around the barrels each time to get that imprinted in his mind. Ashley got back on him, but she wasn't able to pick up the lead the first few tries. However, with help using the inside rein and outside leg, she got it.

Once she was able to pick up the lead, she was able to do some slow work correctly. As she went to the first barrel, I had her look over the top of her horse's head to the proper position. I cautioned her about not pulling down, because pulling down makes a person lean, especially a small girl. Once I got her hands elevated, and she gave her horse enough room to get his back end around the barrel, she was able to lope through the pattern smoothly.

I also made her focus on the horse's ears going around the second and third barrels so she wouldn't look down at them.

I let her make a fast run, and the horse worked his first barrel perfectly. Her father commented that that was like the first barrel they used to have.

Points to Consider – Because the horse worked fine at one point and quit working, he was trying to tell his rider something. The rider needed to be aware and listen to her horse.

Also, the pain, combined with where the rider looked and how she held her hands, made the problem twice as bad. Pulling down with hard and rough hands made the horse's mouth hurt worse. A common belief is that the more strength you use, the more you're going to accomplish. Quite frankly, the opposite is true.

Brenda

At 40, Brenda had been running barrels for quite a few years. She felt she was quite accomplished and had essentially come to the clinic to correct, in her words, "a few little problems with my horse."

When I watched Brenda make her first run, she looked at the barrel, pulled her hands down and leaned hard to the inside of the turns. Her horse was a very nice horse, but they hit the first and second barrels. Brenda pulled on the reins to balance in the turns.

When I rode the horse, he felt sound, gave his head both ways and was very receptive. I simply kept my hands elevated, gave the horse a little more room around the barrels and didn't pull on him. I loped him through several times, helping him stay in position, then made a faster run and he worked awesome. When Brenda got back on her horse, I could tell she was completely unaware of her horse's leads and didn't know that her horse cross-fired around the barrels. He cross-fired even going slowly because Brenda leaned down and pulled him right back over the top of the barrel so he had no choice but to cross-fire to move his back end out and around the barrel.

When a rider can't feel her horse's leads and is completely unaware of what the horse's legs are doing, she either has a lack of knowledge or a lack of wanting to improve her riding. She doesn't understand the importance of these skills. She thinks if she learns the mechanics of barrel racing, that's enough. She doesn't realize that to make the mechanics work, she needs the basics first.

As I continued to work with Brenda, her attitude was that it was the horse's fault, and she wanted to blame him. She kept saying, "He just goes in there. He just wants to hit them!"

With that frame of mind, she wasn't going to improve. I continued to work with her for a good 45 minutes trying to make headway, but she continued to do the same thing, make the same mistakes – look at the barrels, drop her hands and lean over. It happened over and over, and the horse kept hitting barrels. I had her take a break, thinking that if it had time to work into Brenda's head, it would soak in. She came back and still hadn't changed one thing.

I couldn't help Brenda and felt bad for the horse.

Points to Consider – If you lean, are unaware of your leads and pull on the reins to stay on, you have a lot of basics to learn. You can always make a difference in how your horse goes around the barrels. Horses do not want to hit barrels. It's usually rider-error or soreness that causes it. Also, it takes a lot of hard work to get out of the habit of giving wrong signals, and an open mind to become a better rider.

Candy

Candy was a 19-year-old college student who'd been running barrels her whole life. She was a good rider but had never really worked on the basics of her runs. Most likely, she'd worked her horse with a lot of hard runs – setting at barrels, running up hard and slamming the horse into the ground.

When she made her first run, she took her horse to the left first, and jerked him hard to check him. He went extremely wide, all the way to the fence on the first. Her second and third were okay.

Candy was a good rider, with good balance. Best of all, she had a great attitude and was very willing to work.

When I got on her horse, a 5-year-old, he was extremely nervous, which told me that he hadn't had a lot of quiet time around the barrels. He couldn't relax and was completely tight and tense.

Dedicated clinic participants come in all sizes and ages.

159

The first thing I did was take off his tie-down and then flex him to the right and left. He gapped his mouth open both directions and was very sensitive about his head, so I sent him to Randy Reidinger to check his mouth. At it turned out, he had a lot of sharp edges. The angle of his mouth was off and had no bit seats, which forced the bit down onto the bars.

Randy worked on him and once his mouth was comfortable, I spent about 20 minutes building his confidence by walking, trotting and loping through the pattern. I realized this horse had never learned to gather to turn the barrel. He not only wouldn't gather, he also sped up going into the turns.

This is fairly common, and it has its roots in the rider's slow work. The barrel racer lopes to the barrel, then turns the horse loose and lets him go faster around the barrel. This is completely backward of what you want to do and teaches the horse to speed up and push with the hind end, rather than collect and shorten his stride for the turn.

The horse was probably pushed too fast too soon. Even though he had a lot of ability, he was never taught how to achieve what was asked of him.

As I worked to the right and left, I collected him lightly with my hands and showed him how to shorten his stride. Once he understood what I was asking, he relaxed and began to enjoy the slow work we were doing.

When Candy got back on him and felt the difference in how relaxed he was, she was completely amazed and said he'd never felt that way to her. She was able to lope him through the barrels, and because she was a very good rider and aware of her leads she was able to slow him down and collect him for the turns. She could then feel when she needed to slow him down rather than ride him to the barrel and expect him to slow down and turn the barrel on his own.

I told Candy to stay on the program with slow work gradually adding speed back to build her horse's confidence on the first barrel. I saw Candy six months after the clinic and the horse was running 2D times. He was still probably not up to his potential – that would likely take another year or so.

Points to consider – If your horse is in the habit of running past a barrel, jerking and setting him might result in a temporary fix for only one or two runs. You have to teach the horse to collect and shorten his stride for the turns. Don't push him so fast that he runs by the barrel.

Also, remember that just because you don't kick doesn't mean you don't ask your horse for speed. Leaning forward is a great cue for encouraging your horse to go fast.

Jerking, often called "checking," makes a horse stiffen even more. If the horse does go by the barrel a stride or two, don't jerk on him and slam him down at the barrel – just finish the turn as correctly as possible. Then go back and help him work on his transition. With slow work, repetition of turning the barrel correctly every time will help instill in the horse that this is where he's supposed to run.

Remember, at any speed, always go slower around the barrel than you do going to the barrel.

Darla

When I watched 10-year-old Darla's run, it was her first on a new horse. She was a very green rider, who didn't know her leads and was a little afraid to even kick her horse into a lope. Fortunately for her, she was riding a finished horse – one that would take care of her and go only as fast as she was ready for. Her parents had done a good job in selecting the horse. He was capable of 2D times but was willing to wait on his young rider. He was something she could grow with.

Initially, she just walked and trotted through the barrels. Later, we worked on her leads and position around the barrels.

Darla came back eight months later and had developed into a great little horse person. She knew her leads. She had learned to cue the horse, and he'd pick up his leads immediately. She had been running in the 2D at barrel races and winning money.

But it was time for a refresher. She was getting rushed in the turns and really pulling on the inside rein. She'd also begun to kick around her turns, and it caused her horse to bow out away from the barrel. In Darla's mind, pulling closer to the barrel and kicking would make him get closer and she'd be faster. Because of this, the horse wasn't in correct position and wasn't running correct patterns.

I had Darla go back though the pattern, doing slow work only. I told her to keep two hands on the reins, sit down in her turns and push down with her tail bone all the way around the turns. Now that she wasn't pulling on the inside rein and kicking around the barrel, her horse stopped coming out wide on

Improving riding skills is at the heart of Charmayne's clinics.

the back side. And because she now used both reins, her horse finished the turns correctly.

When Darla started her slow work, she came to the first barrel in the right lead but stayed in that lead and was incorrect on the second. She'd forgotten about bringing her horse down to a trot after the first barrel to pick up the correct lead for the second. In order for most horses to change leads, they need a little more speed. It's really natural for a horse that's running and slowing down to change leads, but when you're going slow, if you expect them to make a flying lead change, you have to speed up and that's exactly the wrong thing to do going in to the barrel. So it's better to break down to a trot and make the change before you get to the turn. Remember, if you go around the barrel in the wrong lead you can teach your horse to run barrels that way.

I also reminded her about staying an equal distance away from the barrels. In slow work,

she was coming in to the barrel wide and cutting off the back side.

In her runs, she looked down the inside of the horse's neck at the barrel rather than over the top of the horse's head at where she was going. That made for a too-tight approach and caused her horse to drop his shoulder to the inside and come wide off the back side to complete the turn.

Once Darla made the adjustments, her runs immediately began to look a lot better and would only improve!

Points to consider – Darla had a good beginning but was starting to make mistakes as she got more confidence. It just took correcting those mistakes and reminding her of the basics. I helped her understand that smooth runs are faster.

Another note is that a rider is only able to learn so much. When Darla first came to the clinic at a very basic level, she absorbed a lot.

Students get a lot of one-on-one instruction from Charmayne.

Later, as an improved rider, she was able to understand and pick up even more.

Emma

Sixteen-year-old Emma made her run on her 5-year-old. I saw immediately that the horse didn't move right behind. He carried his back feet high in the air and looked lethargic. I couldn't pinpoint if it was hock soreness, but I knew something wasn't right. Emma went through the run at medium speed. She was a good rider and rode light-handed. I couldn't fault the run other than something didn't look right with the horse.

When I got on him, I flexed him to right and left. He wasn't able to flex properly and really rooted his nose. Emma said his teeth had been worked on, but I sent him to our dentist, Randy Reidinger, to check one more time. He said his mouth was fine.

Next, I sent him to our chiropractor Scotty Wilson. He checked his neck and could tell that some vertebrae were fused. He suggested Emma take the horse to her own veterinarian at home, which she did. He X-rayed the horse and found that his neck had been broken. The professionals informed the owners that the situation was extremely dangerous. With compression on the spinal cord, the horse couldn't feel his hindquarters, and, therefore, where his hind legs were. They were lucky that the horse hadn't gone down with Emma.

Emma and her family had a great attitude. They were sad for the horse but so thankful they found out in time, and that Emma hadn't been hurt.

Point to consider – Be diligent in finding the source of your horse's inconsistencies.

Hannah

Twelve-year-old Hannah was a very small girl. Her parents had recently purchased a 1-2D mare for her. When she started to make her run, the mare refused to come in. It took 15 minutes to get her into the arena. At a rodeo or jackpot they would probably have turned her out. She was riding with a Magic Seat, a Velcro® device to hold her in the saddle. When she came in, she looked right at her barrels and pulled down. The horse actually made a pretty nice run although she came wide off the second and third because she cut off all the axis points and tried to turn right on top of the barrel.

When I got on the mare I flexed her right and left, and found her stiff both directions. I sent her to Randy Reidinger, the dentist, and he discovered that her mouth had very sharp points. The sides of her cheeks were cut, there were sores in her mouth and the teeth angles were bad. It was a horrible mouth.

With her mouth corrected, I took her tie-down off so I didn't put her in a bind, and she could carry her head in a more natural position. Loping in slow circles, she had trouble holding her leads.

I still felt she was sore, so I sent her to Scotty Wilson, our chiropractor, to work on. Her neck was in bad shape. A little skittish, she'd pulled back a lot in her life, which caused problems in the neck, as well as her hips.

After Scotty worked on her, she moved more freely, and it was easier for her to hold her leads doing slow work. When I took her through the pattern, she tried to turn on top of the barrels, missing every axis point. However, when I rode her two-handed, I was able to guide her to all the axis points around the barrels. That gave her more confidence.

When Hannah got back on her horse, I had her take off the Velcro® and explained that the device wouldn't allow her to learn proper balance. If she couldn't ride confidently at fast speeds, she wasn't ready to go fast.

Hannah wanted to pull down and that made her body lean to the inside. I had her elevate her hands, sit down in the saddle and look over the top of her horse's head, giving extra room around the barrels.

When Hannah made a run after those adjustments, her mare was much smoother. There was still work to do as Hannah was a little off balance and hung onto the reins due to her reliance on the Magic Seat. She was also still a little rough with her hands, which caused the mare's head to go up. I helped her realize that even though she was small she could do a lot of damage.

As we worked the mare, she became more relaxed. When Hannah made her run the next day, the mare walked into the arena without any help.

Points to Consider – Hannah's hands, body and seat position were bad enough to keep her horse from wanting to come in. Add the condition of the mare's neck and teeth and you can't blame the mare for not wanting to be a barrel horse any more.

Jan

When Jan made her run, her spurs hit her horse in the ribs with every stride. As she went

163

to the first barrel, her horse ran out of control. When she got to the barrel, she leaned over and jerked the reins hard just as she gripped with her legs, squeezing hard with her spurs in her horse's sides.

At each barrel, she went in out of control, riding one-handed, giving her horse no room going into the barrels. She sliced in and came wide of the back side. Jan was in her 50s and about 50 pounds overweight.

The time she could spend with her horse was limited by her eight-to-five job, so she rode when she could. Jan really loved her horse but never realized how hard she was making his life.

She had heavy hands, demonstrated a lack of control, balanced on the reins and her spurs made contact with her horse's sides as she tried to hold on – all of which hurt and confused her horse.

When I rode her horse, he had learned to be hard-mouthed because Jan had pulled on him so much. He hated his job and his mouth and neck were extremely sore from being jerked and going around the barrels carrying the excess weight that was so off balance.

I loped the horse and tried to build some confidence by riding in correct position. He responded by not pulling as much, and he seemed to enjoy his job more.

The horse actually ran a very correct pattern with hardly any pulling or touching at all. In fact, a couple of the girls who helped me at the clinic liked him so much they wanted to buy him.

When Jan got back on, the first thing I did was take off her spurs. Then I had her work on not leaning, maintaining her seat by pushing her tailbone into the saddle, riding with two hands and keeping proper position around the barrels. I also advised her not to go fast until she had better balance.

I had her ride two-handed without pulling on the reins. She had to use her balance and stomach muscles to stay on, something she'd never done.

When Jan came back in to make a run the last day, she was better but still far from perfect, and she was very disgusted with herself. She was embarrassed that she didn't ride any better. I told her that she now had some tools to work with. She decided she would work on her weight, as well.

Points to Consider – Being overweight makes it more difficult to keep your balance, plus your weight hinders the horse. If you're

overweight, it's even more important to have good hands and seat.

Also, Jan had a husband who was fairly negative about what she was doing during the clinic. If you're a spouse or parent, realize that words of encouragement go much farther than tearing a person down. Always remember that building a person up and looking at the positive side are the best things you can do to help. Many people have to deal with too much negativity in their lives to begin with.

Also, be patient with people as they're learning. People, like horses, learn at different speeds. Some of the riders who take the longest to "get it" in the beginning, might make the better riders in the end.

Nancy

When Nancy made a run, I saw that her horse went wide at the first barrel, but the second and third were pretty good. She wasn't really doing anything horrible, but she was pretty heavy-handed.

Nancy was in her 30s and had been running 3D times. When I got on her horse, he was broke really well. He had obviously been started correctly on barrels.

Because the horse would go by the first barrel, Nancy had put a heavy bit on him, which was a combination headgear with a noseband, double-jointed mouthpiece and shanks. It definitely was too much for the horse, who was very light-mouthed. Not only was there too much bit, Nancy also had a tie-down on the horse, and the combo and tie-down were binding. I showed her how, when she pulled, the chain actually pinched into the side of the horse's face.

The reason the horse started going past the barrel in the first place was that Nancy had lost her position. She was going in one-handed, looking right at the barrel and trying to lift her horse all the way rather than riding two-handed and keeping her position.

I took off the tie-down and combo and put a light gag bit on him. I rode him in proper position, and the horse worked the first barrel fine.

When Nancy got back on, I showed her how to be light with her hands and keep her proper position going to the barrel guiding with two hands. Looking over her horse's head, she was able to maintain the right position going to the first and the horse didn't go wide.

Points to consider – Never upgrade a bit to fix a problem, such as running by the barrel. Move to a bigger bit only for lift or to keep the horse from bending too much.

Patricia

Patricia, 35, had been riding for about 10 years and thought herself an expert on anything to do with barrel racing. She knew all the quick-fix tricks – like running to the barrel and jerking the horse to a stop, or running around the barrel very fast five or six times. Sometimes, she'd go slowly to the barrel, then kick and whip around it.

She did everything she could to scare and ruin a horse, even though, in her mind, she was making him better. On top of that, she whipped her horse over the head when she made a bad run or whipped him out back of the arena when she was finished. She would starve her horses and not water them. She fed the horse she brought to the clinic hay only once a day and no grain to "calm her down."

In her run in the clinic, she came from as far back as she could, running hard to the first barrel. Her horse started to commit to turn, but then ran up the fence. This was a horse that had been a solid 1D horse when she bought it.

She got to the fence, jerked the mare, made her back up and ran her around the first barrel four times. As I talked on the loudspeaker trying to get her to slow down, she was already in a rage. She took off, whipping and kicking to the second barrel, then turned the horse too fast. The horse had no room to get her back end around, so she hit the barrel. It was pretty much the same thing at the third.

I got on the horse, and I could tell it was lame in the front end. The horse couldn't even lope around the barrels collected. It was frantic, tried to turn on top of the barrels and couldn't hold its leads all the way around a barrel.

Patricia wasn't concerned that I thought her horse was sore. I didn't want to ride the mare very long because I felt she was hurting.

When Patricia got back on her horse, he tensed up immediately. I worked with her to get her to ride softer and more relaxed. Her body was so tight her shoulders were up to her ears. I showed her how to relax her shoulders and how to work her mare around the barrels, giving her room and not pulling on her so much

I made a little progress with Patricia on slow work. It was tough because she had the attitude that all the problems were the mare's fault and not hers.

Solving problems through slow work is a hallmark of Charmayne's training philosophy.

In her clinics, Charmayne observes each horse-and-rider team and then makes recommendations based on their individual needs.

With problems addressed and all systems on go, Charmayne lets her students put it all together with a fast run. Although most students see some improvements at the clinic, the biggest benefit comes after they go home and put Charmayne's principles into practice, day after day, retraining their responses and reflexes.

Patricia ended up selling the horse to a girl named Tina, and later Tina brought the horse to one of my clinics.

The mare was a lot more relaxed and quiet with Tina but still didn't look well. Her ribs showed, even though Tina had been taking good care of her.

When Tina made a run at the clinic, the horse went up the fence, just as before. I was more convinced than ever that something was wrong. I told her to take the mare out of the clinic and find what was wrong with her right front leg. I also suggested she have her scoped for ulcers.

She let me know later in the week that the mare indeed had a tear in her right front tendon, and she had ulcers. The horse needed a blister on the injured leg, plus 90 days off. The vet started her on ulcer medication.

When I saw the mare again, her coat was shiny and slick and her ribs weren't showing. A second ultrasound confirmed that the tendon had healed, so Tina started back with slow work.

When she began to run barrels again, the mare no longer ran up the fence at the first barrel and went back to running in the 1D.

Points to Consider – A bad temper and rage have no place on a horse. Also, don't be quick to blame a horse for mistakes. He might be experiencing health issues that are the root of the problem. Don't starve or mistreat any horse because that's the perfect setup for ulcers, especially when the horse is under the kind of stress Patricia's mare was. Ulcers cause severe pain, and a horse will often try to avoid coming into the arena or will run up the fence as a reaction to the discomfort.

14
THE WINNING ATTITUDE

Becoming a champion barrel racer depends on a complete circle of things you do. First of all, it starts with bonding and communicating with your horse. Then, you have to take care of him, understand and meet his needs and manage and ride him correctly. You also have to be a business person, organizing all the details of horse care and competition. Finally, you have to have the right people on your team, especially when it comes to shoeing and health care.

The people who help you — whether family or friends — need to be on the same program with you. To really be helpful to you, they need to understand the training principles you use. If you follow the program outlined in this book, have them read the book, as well.

169

TIPS

Running for First

There was one thing that helped me win on Scamper. No matter what run I made, in my mind it was for first.

The most pressure I ever felt was my tenth run at the National Finals Rodeo, when Scamper was going for his tenth world championship. I planned to retire him after that. It came down to the last run. The stakes were high, not about money, but about the emotional aspect of it being Scamper's last run for a world championship. To me, it was so much more than running for a gold buckle. I experienced a level of emotion I wasn't used to dealing with day in and day out.

All I had to do that day was leave the barrels up, but I knew I had to run to win — like I had done time after time. However, as one of the last to go in that performance, I was aware that the ground was deep. Urging Scamper forward to the first barrel, I sat down in the saddle, then thought I needed to kick up one more stride because of the deep ground. Scamper felt my indecisiveness, and he hit on his front end. Because I'd let my legs loose to push him on, I nearly fell off and had to literally crawl back on. I hung by my fingernails and barely got over in time for the second barrel. I did leave the barrels up. That kept me in the average and let me win the tenth world championship, but I should've gone in there thinking "go, go, go," rather than quitting a hair early. I should've remembered that my game plan on Scamper was to always "run to win."

Barrel racing happens in split seconds. Horses feel your indecisiveness so you should always be completely certain in your run and in what you're doing.

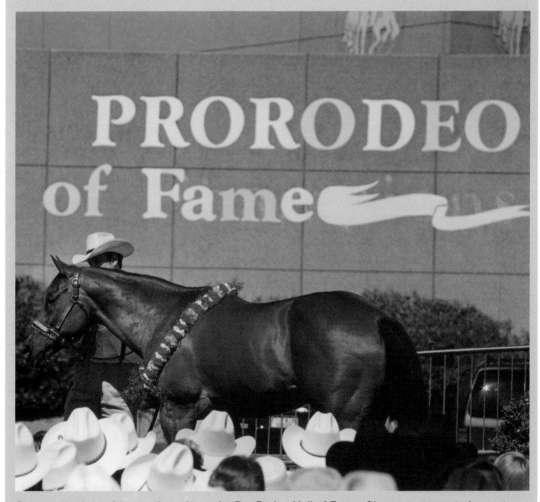

Scamper is shown being inducted into the Pro Rodeo Hall of Fame. Charmayne is an inductee in the National Cowgirl Hall of Fame.

Going the Extra Mile

Barrel racing isn't for the lazy person or the procrastinator. It's time-consuming.

However, it's not enough to have the discipline to work your horse every day. You've got to know when to work and when not to. When your horse is sore or you're suspicious that something is wrong, you have to react quickly and take care of it. If he needs to go to the veterinarian or chiropractor, don't procrastinate or find excuses not to go. It very well might take a lot of time or be far to drive; it all depends on how badly you want to win.

One barrel racer I know has had a lot of good horses, and she's been to the Finals in the lower end of the qualifiers. She'll drive all night and work her horses when she gets to the event. She does put in some effort, but if she'd really focused, several of her horses could've been top five in the world. She just didn't really take care of them and really wouldn't do what it took because it was extra work. She was content with where she was, and that's not a winning attitude.

The problem was that she might feed her horses their morning meal at noon and take their blankets off about that time of day, too, when it was 70 degrees. Sometimes, I'd see that there was no water in their stalls. She had good feed and supplements with her, but, if you don't feed on a schedule and the horses stand around stressing because they don't have anything in their bellies and nothing do drink, that great feed isn't getting used.

It just comes down to not taking care of the horses' needs.

Many barrel racers get in late at night somewhere and put their horses into stalls, without hay, and then go to bed. The next morning — first thing — they give them grain. The horses might look okay, but they're probably not healthy. They might have ulcers because they go for long periods of time without anything in their stomachs, then they get big feedings morning and night. Those horses just crash.

There are so many people who don't put out the effort, or they put out a good bit of effort but that's it. If you've already sacrificed so much, what's a little more? Often that extra effort is the tipping point that helps you move to the next level.

Avoid Negativity

You've got to be strong, knowing that there are many people out there who will be negative

At the top level of competition wait fantastic rewards for those dedicated enough to go for them.

about what you're trying to do. In the past when I was getting with Cruiser, there was one friend who did nothing but run down my horses to my face. He'd tell me Cruiser wasn't any good. I finally had to stop being around him to get away from the negative input.

You have to protect yourself from negativity. Find the positive in things that happen, no matter how bad they are at the time. One of the worst things that ever happened to me was losing Bardo, but because of that Scamper came into my life.

It's so important to surround yourself with positive people and sometimes those closest to you are well-intentioned, but off base. Think about what you're hearing.

One year at the Finals, a family member came in and told my Mom, "Charmayne's not riding like she was." Since she was family, Mom was concerned that she was right. In reality, though, the ground was bad and Scamper was running cautious.

I had been and was still working on my riding, trying to get better, and there were people who, all of a sudden, had all the answers without thinking to ask me. I'm the only one who understood that Scamper was running a little cautious for a good reason. Plus, in the finals the draw order is rotated so that your position on the ground improves two spots each night. I knew Scamper would feel the ground getting better and he would start running better. The point is, those kinds of remarks come from people looking in from the outside, even though they have good intentions.

Another time a guy called my Dad at the Finals and told him Scamper wasn't running like he normally does. He had some advice on what we should do to him. But what he didn't know is that Scamper had had an injury six weeks earlier and needed some runs to get sharp again. My times were good, but I just didn't place in the first few go-rounds.

People who are really trying to help will ask, "What do you think? How does that feel?" They'll dig into your information base to help find out what's going on. However, someone who just sees from the outside and listens to the television commentators only knows half the story.

It's the same at all levels. When you compete at jackpots and someone sees you every fifth jackpot, they still have an opinion on your horse or on how you're riding. But they're on the outside looking in. They don't know how the horse feels, what you're doing or have done. That's why I ride every horse at my clinics, so I know for sure what the rider is experiencing. If you're going to have an opinion, you need to know what you're talking about.

I had people make fun of me in the beginning — how I looked, Scamper's long hair and the green fuzzy saddle pad I had at first. Then

TIPS

Etiquette on the Road

Strive to be a class act in your barrel racing career. Common sense, polite behavior and good, old-fashioned etiquette go a long way in giving our sport a good name. Here are some rules to live and compete by:

Trailering: If you haul with someone, ask them where they tie their horse, and where they would like you to tie yours. Don't just grab the most convenient spot. Likewise with the stalls in the trailer — let them have priority in choosing space.

Parking: When you park, give other people space. Don't pull up next to someone so close that they can't tie their horses.

Warm-up: Be courteous in the warm-up pen. Don't whip, jerk or run around the arena as fast as you can. Not only is it annoying to the other riders, but it also can be very dangerous. If you have a horse that kicks, keep it out of high-traffic areas and let people know. If you knock down a barrel in the warm-up pen, get off your horse and pick it up.

Alley: Keep the alley clear unless you're up. Be courteous to the person who's making a run or is next to go.

Run: During your competition run, if you hit a barrel or make a mistake, finish the run and do your training at home, rather than taking up time and using the ground to tune on your horse. It's better for the horse and more courteous to the rider who's waiting to come in.

Mistakes: Also, if you make an error, don't lose your temper in front of the crowd. It makes all of us look bad. Study and know your horse and understand what's happening. Horses make mistakes. So do you. You might stumble walking up the steps. It doesn't mean you don't know how to walk up a set of steps. It just means you made an error.

Event management: Don't constantly criticize event management. You made the choice to come to the barrel race. If it's not up to your expectations, don't go back.

it was my funny hat. Our style was not the normal look. As I got going, I heard over and over, that the only reason I ever won was because of Scamper, which was true, but they discredited my knowledge of how to ride him and take care of him. I don't feel I ever broke the stigma that I was a good barrel racer until I won the eleventh world title on Cruiser — and even then some still thought I was riding Scamper. What all that means is nothing.

It doesn't matter what people who don't know you and don't care about you think.

Sometimes we beat ourselves by buying in to little things with our horse, as well. Don't let minor issues with a horse frustrate you and ruin his attitude toward you. I once watched a girl as she walked back to her trailer on her horse. As she dismounted, her horse got excited to see the other horse at the trailer, and wanted to get over and smell him. She yelled, "Stop it!" She was trying to discipline him, but in reality she made him want to get away from her even more. He associated stress with her, which made him want comfort from his friends all the more. The first thing horse buddies who haven't seen each other in a while do is acknowledge one another. Do you want your horse's spirit so completely gone he doesn't even get glad to see buddies? That's not what makes a great horse. Every great horse I ever had was full of life, and I let them be who they were as individuals. They weren't slaves.

Likewise, don't let minor issues with people get you down. Don't pick fights. Some people feel that if they don't say or do something when they disagree with someone, they'll pop. They want to bail in and argue about everything. So what if someone else is right? Cut down on your own stress by not buying into those conflicts.

Be Not Afraid

Do you get so scared at a jackpot that you want to throw up? Barrel racing should be something you enjoy, so you've got to learn to focus, in spite of the adrenalin and your churning stomach. One way to get past it is to think about what's making you so nervous.

When I was young, I had a hard time holding Scamper in the alley. My biggest fear was that he'd take off into the arena when someone else was running because when he'd see an open arena, he'd just bolt to it.

That made me more nervous than the actual run. What if I couldn't hold him? I'd

TIPS

When Times Get Tough

- Work hard and stay focused on your priorities.
- Eliminate contact with negative people.
- Eliminate negative activities.
- Look for the positive. Teach yourself not to let things get you down and don't be thin-skinned. Stay on course.

have been embarrassed and horrified and felt bad for the person whose run I messed up.

But knowing what made me nervous helped me identify what my fear was and approach it in a way that I didn't let it happen. He actually never did it, thank goodness.

I'd try to never let him get into a position where he could get away from me and whenever he'd take off toward the alley I'd manage to get him turned.

When you're young like that you can't conceive of being embarrassed that badly. Today, I don't think it would bother me other than feeling badly about the other person. I'd just think, "Well, it happened. Do I have to pay a fine?"

The point, though, is my fear made me keep it from happening. The fear — once identified — helped me prevent a bad circumstance.

What is your fear? Identify it and let that fear drive you to work on your riding skills.

Do you have fear of speed? Fear of not enough control? Fear of what could happen?

Identify the fear then figure out a plan to make your fear not come true.

There are people running barrels who are afraid of falling off. Gripped on to the saddle and to the horse, they hinder the horse the whole way, and they transmit fear to horse. To the best of your ability, keep your body relaxed

Johnette Norris is a big part of Charmayne James, Inc. and runs her clinic business.

and keep your horse relaxed and supple so he can perform.

Are you afraid of hitting a barrel? Think of the good run — the perfect run. Don't let that fear get so big that it's all you think about. Control your mind.

Making It Look Easy

People often tell me that I make barrel racing look easy. I hope I do. But it's actually not that easy. Don't think that making it look easy means I don't work at it. Actually, working at it is what makes it look easy.

In my opinion, the best riders are the ones who ride quietly and make it look effortless.

One day at a rodeo, I was watching the barrel race with some calf ropers. An NFR qualifier rode in. She was hard on horses. She could take the best horse in the world and ruin it in a year. As soon as the horse made one mistake, she was all over it. He'd be so confused and stressed that he'd quit working.

She rode into the arena, spurring and kicking with an outside foot in the horse's shoulder, leaning way to the outside. One of the calf ropers said, "Man, that girl can ride."

As it states plainly on the barn, Chamayne's mission is to help all the barrel racers and barrel horses she can.

TIPS

What Motivates A Champion?

My Dad let us kids work for our money – from the time we were little, we'd clock in and work at the feedyard. We also raised baby calves. When I saw how much you could win rodeoing, I thought I could buy a new truck. That was my motivation in the beginning – not that everything was about money – but it kind of motivates us all.

As time went on with Scamper, I was motivated by how long can we do this and how long can we stay at the top? Each year got more serious because I didn't want to break that run.

In the post-Scamper days, my motivation was to learn everything I could about barrel racing. I knew I wasn't experienced about riding other barrel horses so I crawled on every barrel horse I could ride to figure out what made them work. That, in turn, motivated me to make it to the Finals on other horses and to win the world on Cruiser.

These days, I'm motivated not only by the business aspects of my life but also by helping people with their horses. There's so much misinformation about barrel racing out there. I'm inspired to show people that there's a better way and to try to be an advocate for the horses. I see so many horses that are frustrated and misused.

However, throughout my life and barrel racing career, my deepest motivation has always been internal. It was never to impress people because you can wear yourself out trying to live up to people's expectations. Being a winner can last or not, but knowing that you've given it everything you have does last.

That's what people perceive. But in reality, she'd have better runs and her horses would last longer if she'd ride quieter and kinder.

These days I'm devoted to teaching barrel racers to improve. In recent years, I've been able to establish my schools and clinics. I've always thought that I had the ability to teach, and I have a passion to show people a different way.

It's gratifying when I hear that one of my students won a barrel race and six months later she's still winning.

If I can continue to help students understand their horses better, they can stay winners. It's not about a gimmick or a trick to get by a run. Staying a winner depends on taking care of your horse's health, shoeing, nutrition, conditioning and preparation as much as it does riding into the arena and making a run.

Conducting clinics has been very rewarding for me. I'm blessed that doing the clinics is so easy, thanks in large part to Johnette Norris. Johnette has been my friend for years, and now she manages my clinics. Since she's a barrel racer, too, she understands a lot of our students' concerns and priorities and works with me to try to help them the most.

I love getting emails from clinic participants on how their horses have improved. It's my hope that there are fewer horses confused or upset because of what I've shown you in this book. Please let me hear from you. E-mail me at info@charmaynejames.com.

Qualifying for the National Finals Rodeo is a dream; winning the world is a fairy tale. The whole world knows the special story of a 14-year-old girl and a bay horse that, in 1984, burst onto the rodeo scene and won against the professionals. Charmayne James and Scamper (Gills Bay Boy) earned the Women's Professional Rodeo Association World Championship that year. Then they re-wrote every barrel racing record ever set, keeping a 10-year stranglehold on the title and passing the million dollar mark in earnings.

15

PROFILE OF A CHAMPION

Nineteen consecutive National Finals Rodeo qualifications are a testimony to strength and determination. Like super-stars in any sport, Charmayne James has the iron will and the ability to stay focused to keep sight of the goal at all times.

To Charmayne, it makes perfect sense to spend an hour a day, every day, for something that might make a tenth-second difference in a run. Spending five hours a day for a possible half-second is just doing the math.

At first, she won because she had a great horse. But, even without Scamper, she qualified for the National Finals Rodeo nine times, and won close to a million dollars on four other horses. She also won a world

Gloria, Charmayne and Charles James at the 1987 National Finals Rodeo.

A collection of the buckles Chamayne won before she turned pro.

championship and reserve world championship on Cruiser, a horse she trained.

Charmayne kept winning because she wouldn't allow herself not to win. Initially, that meant doing whatever it took to keep a great horse sound and willing to work. Then, it meant continuing to learn so she could elevate another horse to gold-buckle level.

The first world title was a testament to the love of a young girl for a great horse. The eleventh was proof positive that Charmayne James was a winner, with Scamper or without.

Her winning mindset began early. Charmayne was the youngest of four daughters born to Charles and Gloria James. The family lived in Clayton, New Mexico, and their feedlot, Clayton Cattle Feeders, became the perfect home for a horse-crazy youngster. All she

wanted to do was to be around horses, and the feedlot offered unlimited opportunities.

She was an A and B student, was involved in basketball and track and showed 4-H steers until her life changed at age 14. She was a ninth grader when she and Scamper won their first world championship. From her sophomore year on, she did her schooling through a correspondence school based in Chicago.

Charmayne's history with her horses is recounted, in her words, in Chapter 12, "The Horses." In rodeo, there's never been a more successful competitor.

But records are just a way of keeping score and true champions are always looking ahead. Today, Charmayne is just as dedicated to building her clinic and breeding and training operations as she once was to winning world titles.

The single-minded determination that once thrilled thousands has new directions and a new focus. Charmayne and her husband, Tony Garritano, welcomed the birth of their son, Tyler Anthony, on May 11, 2004. This singular event changed her life forever, and she says that her son is worth more than all her titles and acclaim. Predictably, she takes him with her everywhere, and her 2004 and 2005 clinics were often temporarily interrupted with a 15-minute break while she tended to Tyler.

She moves deliberately, talks softly and spends time each day with her horses. They're still one of her main priorities. More than the titles, more than the accolades, Charmayne's horses continue to come first.

Through past success and new goals, Charmayne remains positive, personable, quiet and deeply rooted in the principles of hard work. She still believes that dreams come true, whether dreams of arena accomplishment or of business success.

At one clinic, it was after 8:00 p.m. on a day that had begun 12 hours earlier. Most students had already left and staff members were tired, impatient to call it a day. Charmayne had ridden every horse in the clinic, and worked with every rider. Progress had been noted and applauded.

But one student just didn't get it. Maybe it was nerves, maybe an inability to respond to coaching. She had worked earlier in the day to no success. Charmayne had her come back for one more session.

It was hot, dusty and late, yet Charmayne patiently repeated the instructions, and each time the girl worked her horse through them. There was nothing in Charmayne's voice to show

how exhausted she must have been, and no intonation of impatience with the frustrated rider.

Once, then again and again and again, the rider made the same mistake.

Her coach never waivered, repeating the instructions over and again, along with encouragement, "You can do this."

And she did, finally, after hours or failure.

A big smile spread over Charmayne's face. "Okay, let's do it one more time to make sure you have it now!"

A perfect repetition later and the day was finally over. It was another success for the champion, maybe not the kind that wins titles, but the kind that means the most to her now.

Charmayne James is the most decorated female equestrian athlete of all time and her fans span three generations. They admire her drive and enthusiasm as a successful athlete, business woman and mother. Although Charmayne retired in 2003 from rodeoing full-time, she remains an icon of the sport.

The records are seemingly endless and they began from the age of 14, for the woman who would one day become the all-time leading money earner in the sport of barrel racing. She holds the record for the most professional barrel racing world championships at 11 and the most consecutive Women's Professional Rodeo Association world championships, with

10. She was the first Women's Professional Rodeo Association member to earn the elite #1 back number at the National Finals Rodeo, in 1987, when her year-long earnings surpassed that of any Professional Rodeo Cowboys Association All-Around cowboy.

Charmayne was the first WPRA member listed in the *Guinness Book of World Records* (1987 and 1992) and holds the record for the most consecutive National Finals Rodeo qualifications for men or woman, with 19. She's also the holder of more individual world championships than any other woman in professional sports.

Charmayne's wedding was a time for family to come together. From Left, Eugenie Crist (sister), Bernadette Mussel (sister), Charmayne, Elizabth Rothwell (niece) and her daughter, Taylor, Georgina Trygg (sister).

Charmayne, Tyler and Tony Garritano

A Record of Achievement

1984
Age 14 • Arena winnings $53,499

Houston Rodeo championship — first year
Rookie of the Year — Women's Professional Rodeo Association
Wrangler Series champion

Dodge Series champion
National Finals Rodeo champion
World Champion barrel racer

ALL NFR PHOTOS BY KENNETH SPRINGER

BY SPRINGER

1985 • *Age 15* • *Arena winnings $93,847*

Houston Rodeo championship – second year
Coors Chute Out champion
Winston Pro Tour champion
Wrangler Series champion
Dodge Series champion
World Champion barrel racer

1986 • *Age 16* • *Arena winnings $151,969*

Houston Rodeo championship – third year
Turquoise Circuit champion
Leading money winner in pro rodeo - men and women
Coors Chute Out champion
Winston Series champion
Winston Pro Tour champion
Wrangler Series champion
Dodge Series champion
National Finals Rodeo champion
World Champion barrel racer
Inducted into Panhandle Sports Hall of Fame,
   Amarillo, Texas

1987 • *Age 17* • *Arena winnings $120,002*

Houston Rodeo championship – fourth year
Turquoise Circuit champion
Leading season money winner in sport of pro rodeo
First woman in history to wear #1 going into competi-
   tion at the National Finals Rodeo
Coors Chute Out champion
Coors Barrel Racing champion
Wrangler Bonus NFR champion
Wrangler Series champion
National Finals Rodeo champion
World Champion barrel racer

1988 • *Age 18* • *Arena winnings $130,540*

Houston Rodeo championship – fifth year
1988 Calgary Olympics – gold medal team
Dodge Series champion
Coors Chute Out champion
World Champion barrel racer

181

1989 • *Age 19* • *Arena winnings $96,651*

Houston Rodeo championship – sixth year
Coors Chute Out champion
Dodge Series champion
AQHA Horse of the Year
Sierra Circuit champion
National Finals Rodeo champion
World Champion barrel racer

1990 • *Age 20* • *Arena winnings $130,328*

First Million Dollar Cowgirl
Coors Chute Out champion
Dodge Series champion
AQHA Horse of the Year
Wrangler Series champion
Copenhagen / Skoal Series champion
National Finals Rodeo champion
World Champion barrel racer

1991 • *Age 21* • *Arena winnings $130,328*

Houston Rodeo championship – seventh year
U.S. Team Roping Championship – California champion
Coors Chute Out champion
Dodge Series champion
Crown Royal season winner
Wrangler World of Rodeo champion
Sierra Circuit champion
AQHA Horse of the Year
World Champion barrel racer

1992 • *Age 22* • *Arena winnings $110,867*

Houston Rodeo championship – eighth year
Inducted into National Cowgirl Hall of Fame,
    Hereford, Texas
Calgary Stampede champion
Crown Royal season winner
World Champion barrel racer

By
SPRINGER

1993 • *Age 23 Arena winnings $103,609*

Houston Rodeo championship – ninth year
Crown Royal season winner
Dodge Series champion
National Finals Rodeo champion
World Champion barrel racer

1994

Age 24 • Arena winnings $67,504

Houston Rodeo championship – tenth year

Crown Royal season winner
National Finals Rodeo qualifier

1995 • *Age 25 • Arena winnings $50,345*

Sierra Circuit champion
National Finals Rodeo qualifier
Inducted into National Cowboy Hall of Fame,
   Oklahoma City, Oklahoma

1996 • *Age 26 • Arena winnings $49,995*

Pacific Cutting Horse Association – Reno
   Stakes champion
Dodge National Circuit Finals champion
National Finals Rodeo qualifier
Scamper inducted into Pro Rodeo Hall of Fame,
   in Colorado Springs, Colorado

1997
Age 27 • Arena winnings $54,442

Tucson Rodeo barrel racing champion – new arena record
Dodge National Circuit Finals champion

National Finals Rodeo Qualifier – 14 consecutive years
Fastest time award – 1997 NFR

1998
Age 28 • Arena winnings $116,325
Finished fifth in the world standings
National Finals Rodeo qualifier

1999
Age 29 • Arena winnings $88,520
Finished sixth in the world standings
National Finals Rodeo qualifier

2000
Age 30 • Arena winnings $146,000
WPRA Reserve World Champion
Winter Tour Finals champion
National Finals Rodeo qualifier

2001
Age 31 • Arena winnings $129,270
Finished third in world standings
National Finals Rodeo qualifier

By SPRINGER

2002

Age 32 • Arena winnings $186,405

Finished first world standings
Winner of the USST Winter Finale
Jack Daniels World Standings year-end season leader
Leader of USST Wrangler Summer Tour points
Set arena record at Ellensburg, Washington
Set arena record at Pendleton, Oregon

Fastest time at Cheyenne, Wyoming
Fastest time at Salinas, California
NFR average winner
WPRA World Champion
Inductee into the Texas Cowboy Hall of Fame,
    Fort Worth, Texas

Although Charmayne is now retired from competitive WPRA Barrel Racing, she's very much the leader in the promotion of women's equine activities. The following are partnership and business ventures she's involved with:

Barrel Horse News

Monthly guest columnist for the leading barrel horse magazine in the country.

www.charmaynejames.com

Business centers around the Charmayne James Web site. Web site averages 550,000 hits per month and an average of 28,000 unique visitors per month.

Morinda Corporation

(Tahitian Noni Equine Essentials) Leading spokesperson; featured in print and television, and attends speaking engagements on behalf of Morinda.

Scamper's Choice Premium Horse Feed

Debuted in fall of 2005. The feed formula that took Scamper and Cruiser to 11 world titles. Available nationwide.

Rocky Mountain Clothing

Endorses a signature line of clothing.

Circle M Trailers

Offers Platinum Coach Trailers.

Professional's Choice

Developed the Professional's Choice "Charmayne James" equine equipment line of goods and services.

Charmayne James "Record Breaker" and "Scamper" Saddles

Developed by Charmayne to fit the horse and help the rider maintain a good seat.

National Finals Rodeo

Featured in nationally broadcast commercials.

Equine Affaire

Featured speaker at leading equine expositions in California, Massachusetts and Ohio.

Competitions

Enters various local and regional competitions and rodeos.

Publications

Barrel Horse News
Elle
Glamour
LIFE Magazine
People
PRCA and WPRA News
Quarter Horse Journal
Quarter Horse News
Ropers Sports News
Seventeen
Sports Illustrated
US
USA Today
Western Horseman

Television

ABC Sunday News with Sam Donaldson
ABC Wide World of Sports
Amazing World of Guinness
America's Horse
CBS Morning Show
Discovery Channel
ESPN
Good Morning America
PM Magazine

PROFILE:
CHERYL MAGOTEAUX

Cheryl Magoteaux has quite a few credentials to write a book on barrel racing. The former college horsemanship instructor is a past Women's Professional Rodeo Association National Champion in barrel racing. As a Women's National Finals qualifier, she garnered major team roping and barrel racing event wins, including at the prestigious North American Livestock Exposition, held in Louisville, Kentucky.

Cheryl has written, edited and photographed for a wide range of publications, earning national awards and recognition for both her writing and photography. She's also done color commentary for Waltenberry's Reining Video Monthly.

Her company, Pro Management, provides management, advertising, publishing, media and publicity services for some of the giants in the western horse industry – the National Reining Breeders Classic (NRBC) and the National Reined Cow Horse Association (NRCHA). Pro Management also publishes over a dozen publications each year, including the NRCHA's official bi-monthly magazine, *Stock Horse News*.

The company also oversees the production of the NRBC, the world's largest added-money reining, and all the NRCHA's premier events, including the NRCHA Snaffle Bit Futurity. Another high-profile event is the Fiesta in the Park, which hosts the United States Equestrian Federation Reining Championship.

Magoteaux's offices are located on her ranch in Byars, Oklahoma, which is also home to a commercial cattle operation and a barn full of barrel horses. Cheryl and her daughter, Savannah, enjoy attending rodeos and barrel racing events, where Savannah is an avid competitor.

Books Published by
WESTERN HORSEMAN®

ARABIAN LEGENDS by Marian K. Carpenter
280 pages and 319 photographs. Abu Farwa, *Aladdinn, *Ansata Ibn Halima, *Bask, Bay-Abi, Bay El Bey, Bint Sahara, Fadjur, Ferzon, Indraff, Khemosabi, *Morafic, *Muscat, *Naborr, *Padron, *Raffles, *Raseyn, *Sakr, Samtyr, *Sanacht, *Serafix, Skorage, *Witez II, Xenophonn.

BARREL RACING, Completely Revised by Sharon Camarillo
128 pages, 158 photographs and 17 illustrations. Teaches foundation horsemanship and barrel racing skills for horse and rider, with additional tips on feeding, hauling and winning.

CALF ROPING by Roy Cooper
144 pages and 280 photographs. Complete coverage of roping and tying.

CHARMAYNE JAMES ON BARREL RACING
by Charmayne James with Cheryl Magoteaux
192 pages and over 200 color photograps. Charmayne shares the training techniques and philosophy that made her the most successful barrel racer in history. Also included are vignettes of horses and riders that illustrate Charmayne's approach to indentifying and correcting problems in barrel racing, as well as examples and experiences from over 20 years as a world-class competitor in this exciting event.

COWBOYS & BUCKAROOS by Tim O'Byrne
176 pages and over 250 color photograps. The author, who's spent 20 years on ranches and feedyards, explains in great detail the trade secrets and working lifestyle of this North American icon. Readers can follow the cowboy crew through the four seasons of a cattle-industry year, learn their lingo and the Cowboy Code they live by, understand how they start colts, handle cattle, make long circles in rough terrain and much, much more. Many interesting sidebars, including excerpts from the author's personal journal offering firsthand accounts of the cowboy way.

CUTTING by Leon Harrel
144 pages and 200 photographs. Complete guide to this popular sport.

FIRST HORSE by Fran Devereux Smith
176 pages, 160 black-and-white photos, numerous illustrations. Step-by-step information for the first-time horse owner and/or novice rider.

HELPFUL HINTS FOR HORSEMEN
128 pages and 325 photographs and illustrations. WH readers and editors provide tips on every facet of life with horses and offer solutions to common problems horse owners share. Chapters include: Equine Health Care; Saddles; Bits and Bridles; Gear; Knots; Trailers/Hauling Horses; Trail Riding/Backcountry Camping; Barn Equipment; Watering Systems; Pasture, Corral and Arena Equipment; Fencing and Gates; Odds and Ends.

IMPRINT TRAINING by Robert M. Miller, D.V.M.
144 pages and 250 photographs. Learn to "program" newborn foals.

LEGENDS 1 by Diane Ciarloni
168 pages and 214 photographs. Barbra B, Bert, Chicaro Bill, Cowboy P-12, Depth Charge (TB), Doc Bar, Go Man Go, Hard Twist, Hollywood Gold, Joe Hancock, Joe Reed P-3, Joe Reed II, King P-234, King Fritz, Leo, Peppy, Plaudit, Poco Bueno, Poco Tivio, Queenie, Quick M Silver, Shue Fly, Star Duster, Three Bars (TB), Top Deck (TB) and Wimpy P-1.

LEGENDS 2 by Jim Goodhue, Frank Holmes, Phil Livingston, Diane Ciarloni
192 pages and 224 photographs. Clabber, Driftwood, Easy Jet, Grey Badger II, Jessie James, Jet Deck, Joe Bailey P-4 (Gonzales), Joe Bailey (Weatherford), King's Pistol, Lena's Bar, Lightning Bar, Lucky Blanton, Midnight, Midnight Jr, Moon Deck, My Texas Dandy, Oklahoma Star, Oklahoma Star Jr., Peter McCue, Rocket Bar (TB), Skipper W, Sugar Bars and Traveler.

LEGENDS 3 by Jim Goodhue, Frank Holmes, Diane Ciarloni, Kim Guenther, Larry Thornton, Betsy Lynch
208 pages and 196 photographs. Flying Bob, Hollywood Jac 86, Jackstraw (TB), Maddon's Bright Eyes, Mr Gun Smoke, Old Sorrel, Piggin String (TB), Poco Lena, Poco Pine, Poco Dell, Question Mark, Quo Vadis, Royal King, Showdown, Steel Dust and Two Eyed Jack.

LEGENDS 4
216 pages and 216 photographs. Several authors chronicle the great Quarter Horses Zantanon, Ed Echols, Zan Parr Bar, Blondy's Dude, Diamonds Sparkle, Woven Web/Miss Princess, Miss Bank, Rebel Cause, Tonto Bars Hank, Harlan, Lady Bug's Moon, Dash For Cash, Vandy, Impressive, Fillinic, Zippo Pine Bar and Doc O' Lena.

LEGENDS 5 by Frank Holmes, Ty Wyant, Alan Gold, Sally Harrison
248 pages, including about 300 photographs. The stories of Little Joe, Joe Moore, Monita, Bill Cody, Joe Cody, Topsail Cody, Pretty Buck, Pat Star Jr., Skipa Star, Hank H, Chubby, Bartender, Leo San, Custus Rastus (TB), Jaguar, Jackie Bee, Chicado V and Mr Bar None.

LEGENDS 6 by Frank Holmes, Patricia Campbell, Sally Harrison, GloryAnn Kurtz, Cheryl Magoteaux, Heidi Nyland, Bev Pechan, Juli S. Thorson
236 pages, including about 270 photographs. The stories of Paul A, Croton Oil, Okie Leo Flit Bar, Billietta, Coy's Bonanza, Major Bonanza, Doc Quixote, Doc's Prescription, Jewels Leo Bar, Colonel Freckles, Freckles Playboy, Peppy San, Mr San Peppy, Great Pine, The Invester, Speedy Glow, Conclusive, Dynamic Deluxe and Caseys Charm

NATURAL HORSE-MAN-SHIP by Pat Parelli
224 pages and 275 photographs. Parelli's six keys to a natural horse-human relationship.

PROBLEM-SOLVING, Volume 1 by Marty Marten
248 pages and over 250 photos and illustrations. Develop a willing partnership between horse and human — trailer-loading, hard-to-catch, barn-sour, spooking, water-crossing, herdbound and pull-back problems.

PROBLEM-SOLVING, Volume 2 by Marty Marten
A continuation of Volume 1. Ten chapters with illustrations and photos.

RAISE YOUR HAND IF YOU LOVE HORSES by Pat Parelli w. Kathy Swan
224 pages and over 200 black and white and color photos. The autobiography of the world's foremost proponent of natural horsemanship. Chapters contain hundreds of Pat Parelli stories, from the clinician's earliest remembrances to the fabulous experiences and opportunities he has enjoyed in the last decade. As a bonus, there are anecdotes in which Pat's friends tell stories about him.

RANCH HORSEMANSHIP by Curt Pate w. Fran Devereux Smith
220 pages and over 250 full color photos and illustrations. Learn how almost any rider at almost any level of expertise can adapt ranch-horse-training techniques to help his mount become a safer more enjoyable ride. Curt's ideas help prepare rider and horse for whatever they might encounter in the round pen, arena, pasture and beyond.

REINING, Completely Revised by Al Dunning
216 pages and over 300 photographs. Complete how-to training for this exciting event.

RIDE SMART, by Craig Cameron w. Kathy Swan
224 pages and over 250 black and white and color photos. Under one title, Craig Cameron combines a look at horses as a species and how to develop a positive, partnering relationship with them, along with good, solid horsemanship skills that suit both novice and experienced riders. Topics include ground-handling techniques, hobble-breaking methods, colt-starting, high performance maneuvers and trailer-loading. Interesting sidebars, such as trouble-shooting tips and personal anecdotes about Cameron's life, complement the main text.

RODEO LEGENDS by Gavin Ehringer
Photos and life stories fill 216 pages. Included are: Joe Alexander, Jake Barnes & Clay O'Brien Cooper, Joe Beaver, Leo Camarillo, Roy Cooper, Tom Ferguson, Bruce Ford, Marvin Garrett, Don Gay, Tuff Hedeman, Charmayne James, Bill Linderman, Larry Mahan, Ty Murray, Dean Oliver, Jim Shoulders, Casey Tibbs, Harry Tompkins and Fred Whitfield.

ROOFS AND RAILS by Gavin Ehringer
144 pages, 128 black-and-white photographs plus drawings, charts and floor plans. How to plan and build your ideal horse facility.

STARTING COLTS by Mike Kevil
168 pages and 400 photographs. Step-by-step process in starting colts.

THE HANK WIESCAMP STORY by Frank Holmes
208 pages and over 260 photographs. The biography of the legendary breeder of Quarter Horses, Appaloosas and Paints.

TEAM PENNING by Phil Livingston
144 pages and 200 photographs. How to compete in this popular family sport.

TEAM ROPING WITH JAKE AND CLAY by Fran Devereux Smith
224 pages and over 200 photographs and illustrations. Learn about fast times from champions Jake Barnes and Clay O'Brien Cooper. Solid information about handling a rope, roping dummies and heading and heeling for practice and in competition. Also sound advice about rope horses, roping steers, gear and horsemanship.

WELL-SHOD by Don Baskins
160 pages, 300 black-and-white photos and illustrations. A horse-shoeing guide for owners and farriers. Easy-to-read, step-by-step how to trim and shoe a horse for a variety of uses. Special attention is paid to corrective shoeing for horses with various foot and leg problems.

WESTERN TRAINING by Jack Brainard
With Peter Phinny. 136 pages. Stresses the foundation for western training.

WIN WITH BOB AVILA by Juli S. Thorson
Hardbound, 128 full-color pages. Learn the traits that separate horse-world achievers from also-rans. World champion horseman Bob Avila shares his philosophies on succeeding as a competitor, breeder and trainer.

Western Horseman, established in 1936, is the world's leading horse publication. For subscription information: 800-877-5278.
To order other *Western Horseman* books: 800-874-6774 • *Western Horseman*, Box 7980, Colorado Springs, CO 80933-7980.
Web site: **www.westernhorseman.com**.